Sparks   1/10/63   (62-7177)

# THE FIRST BATTLE
# OF THE MARNE

GREAT BATTLES SERIES
HANSON W. BALDWIN,
General Editor

Also by ROBERT B. ASPREY
THE PANTHER'S FEAST

# THE FIRST BATTLE OF THE MARNE

*ROBERT B. ASPREY*

## J. B. LIPPINCOTT COMPANY

### PHILADELPHIA & NEW YORK

IN AUGUST AND SEPTEMBER OF 1914 MANY BRAVE SOLDIERS DIED BELIEVING IN THE RIGHT OF THEIR COUNTRIES' WRONGS. THIS BOOK IS DEDICATED TO THEM.

# ACKNOWLEDGMENT

ONE OF THE MOST pleasurable by-products of writing is the people you meet.

The range, particularly in a book of this nature, is tremendous—from the august professor who spurts expertise like a Gatling gun to the quiet Catalan innkeeper who accepts your temper tantrums as a corollary to progress (or lack of it) on your book. A fusty librarian may spend hours, even days, searching out a remote fact for you, an old friend may inconvenience the entire family to put you up, a photo-copier may work overtime to give you the material to take along on tomorrow's plane.

Seemingly everyone transcends nationality and habit to help you in your work, and for this you must be eternally grateful.

Enormously helpful to me in meeting the administrative and research requirements imposed by the writing of this book were, in America: Mr. Robert Haynes and his staff at the Harvard College Library; Mr. Robert W. Krauskopf and his staff at the National Archives; Lieutenant Colonel A. S. Williams, USA, and the Department of the Army; Lieutenant Colonel P. N. Pierce, USMC, and Mr. Michael O'Quinlavan and their staffs at Headquarters, U.S. Marine Corps; Lieutenant Colonel T. N. Greene, USMC, editor and publisher of the *Marine Corps Gazette;* Major James F. Sunderman, USAF, and the Department of the Air Force; Mrs. Martha Holler, Department of Defense; Mr. John Spore, editor of *Army* magazine; the staff of the Library of Congress; in London: Mrs. Joan Saunders of Writer's and Speaker's Research; Brigadier C. N. Barclay, editor of *Army Quarterly;* Brigadier J. Stephenson, Director of the Royal United Service Institution; the staff of the Imperial War Museum, London, and La Musée de l'Armée, Paris; in Bermuda: Mr. Graham Rosser.

For critical reading of the manuscript I wish to thank Lieutenant General M. B. Burrows, Brigadier General S. B. Griffith, II, Marshal of the RAF Sir John Slessor, Captain B. H. Liddell Hart, Mrs. Joan Saunders and Mr. Brian Burland. None of them, of course, is responsible for my errors, interpretations and conclusions, the more so since I did not always take their advice.

For unstinted hospitality and constant encouragement I wish to thank many friends in America, England and Europe. I am particularly indebted in America to Lieutenant Colonel and Mrs. T. W. Flatley and Mr. Lawrence H. McGill; in England to Mr. Brian H. MacDermot; in Spain to Brigadier General and Mrs. S. B. Griffith, II, and to Mr. Leslie Grimes.

As always, my parents, Mr. and Mrs. Peter Asprey, Jr., and my sister, Professor Winifred Asprey, have offered constant help and encouragement.

Finally I wish to thank my editors, Mr. Hanson W. Baldwin and Mr. Stewart Richardson of Lippincott, for their understanding attitude about delayed deadlines, for their perceptive criticisms and suggestions and for their splendid help and encouragement throughout the preparation of this book.

ROBERT B. ASPREY

*Angel Steps Studio*
*Southampton*
*Bermuda*

# CONTENTS

No part of the Great War compares in interest with its opening. The measured silent drawing together of gigantic forces, the uncertainty of their movements and positions, the number of unknown and unknowable facts made the first collision a drama never surpassed. Nor was there any other period in the war when the general battle was waged on so great a scale, when the slaughter was so swift or the stakes so high. Moreover in the beginning our faculties of wonder, horror and excitement had not been cauterized or deadened by the furnace fires of years. In fact the war was decided in the first twenty days of fighting, and all that happened afterwards consisted in battles which, however formidable and devastating, were but desperate and vain appeals against the decision of fate.

—WINSTON S. CHURCHILL
(from the Foreword to *Liaison, 1914* by
Brigadier E. L. Spears)

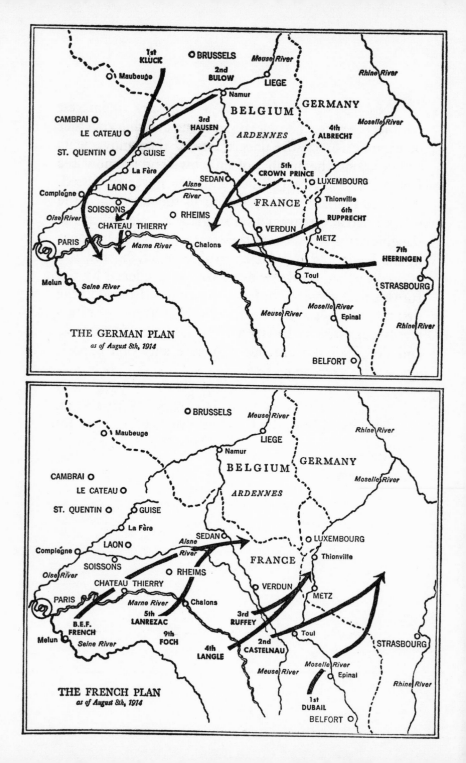

THE GERMAN PLAN
*as of August 8th, 1914*

THE FRENCH PLAN
*as of August 8th, 1914*

# IN THE BEGINNING . . .

1 No GREAT BATTLE stands alone, a tactical monolith separate from the surging forces of either its strategic campaign or its parent war. The origin of each, the plan and purpose, the forces involved, the leadership, the outcome—all belong to a larger scheme of things, a political-military relationship that determines the final importance of a single battle.

Especially is this true of the Battle of the Marne. Fought from September 5–10, 1914, this vast, incredibly complex action climaxed a military campaign begun on August 4 when Germany invaded Belgium in the first great offensive of World War I.

No one could have forecast the Battle of the Marne on the day that German troops marched across the border of Belgium, and no one did forecast it until two days before its premature beginning. Had those first weeks of war seen the forces of either side altered or certain high command orders changed, had they seen fortune smile here or the fog of battle lift there, then the full effect of the Battle of the Marne might well have yielded to an earlier Battle of Lorraine or Battle of Mons, or perhaps later to a Battle of the Seine or a Battle of the Alps.

Any one of these could have resulted from the tactical factors that produced the Battle of the Marne or from the political-strategic factors which underwrote the tactics: the explosion of Europe into a war releasing vast armies long trained to fight under complex plans long conceived to win.

Taken together they spelled immense conflict. The opening of the western war saw a German battle line stretching almost from the Swiss Alps along the French border through Luxembourg past the Belgian and Dutch borders, some 475 miles of mountains, valleys, hills and plains. The major front of the Battle of the Marne covered over 125 miles—from northeast of Paris to Verdun—with five German armies fighting five Allied armies, another four armies engaged from Verdun south to the Alps. The Germans marched to the Marne expecting to finish the war within a week; six days later they began a retreat to trenches where they would remain for four years.

Enormous stakes and meticulous plans made their shock the greater. The storm that broke in August of 1914 had been brewing for years: since 1908 the Triple Alliance of Germany and Austria-Hungary followed by a dejected and wavering Italy had faced the *Entente* of France, Russia and England through crisis after crisis, each settled with increasing difficulty. War now meant an all-out contest to see who would rule Europe, and in 1914 Europe meant the world.

Though based on centuries-old antagonisms and desires, the violent political air of 1914 had its genesis in the aftermath of the Franco-Prussian War of 1870–71 which threw the glove of a new and ambitious German nation into the power ring of Europe and the world.[1]

When Germany emerged victorious from this war her problem lay in consolidating her gains before further expanding her power. Under the aegis of her brilliant if Machiavellian chancellor, Prince Bismarck, she concluded a defensive alliance with her southeastern neighbor, Austria-Hungary, in 1879 and in 1882 enlarged this to the famous Triple Alliance by a treaty with Italy.[2]

Simultaneously Bismarck wove a series of alliances that kept France isolated, particularly from Russia, and kept Austria-Hungary quiet, particularly in the Balkans. The cornerstone of Bismarck's policy, the Three Emperors' Alliance, drew Russia, Austria-Hungary and Germany into common action in all Balkan affairs; in 1887 it was replaced by the famous and very vital Reinsurance Treaty with Russia: a secret agreement, by which each country pledged neutrality if the other went to war, but not if Germany attacked France, or Russia attacked Austria.

Bismarck's subtlety proved too great for either the Chief of the German Great General Staff, Count Waldersee, who wished to fight a preventive war with Russia, or the new Emperor Wilhelm II, who soon after claiming the throne in 1888 allowed himself to be taken in by the anti-Bismarck clique headed by ambitious Baron Holstein.[3] In 1890 Bismarck was dumped, the new chancellor, Caprivi, soon abandoned the Reinsurance Treaty, and Russia found herself standing alone. But not for long. In 1891 she started talks with France which a year later resulted in a military agreement and a Dual Alliance so dreaded by Bismarck.

With the powers of Europe thus divided, albeit loosely, England now emerged as an isolated *x* factor, a position not at all to her liking. Because of her difficulties with Russia in Persia and with France in Egypt, she at first leaned toward an alliance with Germany and in 1902 did align herself with Japan. But Germany's transition from internal consolidation to overseas expansion coupled with her intention to build a powerful navy created increasingly serious incidents which finally drove England to a *rapprochement* with France. Aided by omnipresent French fear of her rapacious neighbor Germany, negotiations between France and England resolved the vexatious colonial question in favor of the 1904 *Entente*, which was strengthened by Germany's threatening attitude during the Algeciras crisis of 1906.[4] This shift in the power struggle cost Germany more than the support of England, whose strong friendship with Italy automatically weakened the latter's allegiance to the Triple Alliance.

Kaiser Wilhelm's increasing friendship with the Czar of Russia, the famous Willy–Nicky relationship, at first offset Germany's loss. But willing as Nicholas was to connive against England, whom he loathed for her part in the Russo-Japanese war of 1904–05, he could not be induced to abandon his agreement with France. Too, Germany's continued attempts at chest-thumping expansion, in this case toward Turkey, cooled the Russian emperor's ardor until finally he began negotiations with England which in 1907 led to an understanding over Persia.[5]

The outlines of the European power picture were now so fully drawn that the Annexation Crisis of 1909 almost exactly anticipated the final political reaction of 1914.[6] When late in 1908 Austria-Hungary suddenly annexed the two Balkan provinces of Bosnia and Herzegovina, Serbia protested and mobilized, Russia backed Serbia, and Germany backed Austria.

The combined action of England and Germany finally averted general war, but the political-military alignment of the 1909 crisis changed only in intensity until the outbreak of the Balkan wars. In a memorandum of 1912 Moltke wrote, "The outbreak of a general war will, as a result of the alliances on both sides, follow on a collision between two of the great powers of Europe."[7] By 1914 the stream of conflict and crisis motivated by the two fountainheads of power, Germany and Austria-Hungary on the one hand, France, Russia and England on the other, had produced a virtually inflexible political situation. Worse yet, the interim years had altered the military readiness of all nations, a process which put far too much power in military hands, far too much hope in military plans.

One incident was as good as another. On the sunny morning of June 28, 1914, a young Serbian student named Gavrilo Prinzip pushed through a crowded Sarajevo street, leaped onto a royal motorcar, fired two shots into a uniformed, bulky body and became the assassin of Archduke Francis Ferdinand, Austria's future emperor.

Shocked by the murder, European diplomats hoped that Austria would not convert it into a *casus belli*. Count Berchtold, Austria's Foreign Minister, whose own position was as shaky as his country's prestige, did exactly this. Backed by Conrad von Hötzendorf, Chief of the Imperial General Staff, who had wanted war against Serbia for years, Berchtold persuaded the old Emperor Francis Joseph to ask Germany to support an aggressive Austrian action. On July 5 Emperor Wilhelm's reply—the famous "blank check"—announced that Austria "could depend on the complete support of Germany."[8]

While the European powers, particularly Germany and Austria, began quiet military preparations, Berchtold on July 23 delivered an ultimatum to Serbia and demanded her reply in forty-eight hours. The extreme insult of the terms, which Serbia could not have accepted without forfeiting her sovereignty, shocked all of Europe, even Kaiser Wilhelm who recovered to reaffirm his military support of Austria the next day. Simultaneously Russia reiterated her support of Serbia, France pledged her aid to Russia, and Sir Edward Grey, England's Foreign Minister, urged Germany to arrange an extension of time for Serbia to answer the Austrian note. This request was ignored as were Grey's frantic attempts in the following days to settle the affair by a conference of European powers. Serbia, however, met the deadline and agreed to all except two of Austria's terms—a conciliatory effort rejected by Austria. On July 28 she declared war on Serbia and began a partial mobilization on the Serbian frontier.

The next three days witnessed a frenzied exchange of formal ultimatums and informal propositions among Berlin, Vienna, St. Petersburg, Rome, Paris and London that at times seemed to hold hope of peace but in the end came to naught.[9] On July 31 Russia ordered general mobilization. Austria followed a few hours later. Germany immediately declared a preliminary mobilization which despite actual mobilization measures and armed raids into France kept from her the stigma of general mobilization while she carried out pathetic and futile last-minute attempts to gain England's neutrality, the more important since Italy on July 31 declared herself neutral.

With general mobilization under way in Russia and Austria nothing in the world could have saved the peace of Europe after July 31. On August 1 Germany declared war against Russia and ordered general mobilization; on August 2 she delivered an ultimatum to Belgium demanding the right to cross Belgian territory; on August 3 she declared war on France; on August 4 German troops crossed the Belgian border.

Europe was at war.

# SCHLIEFFEN, MOLTKE
# AND THE GERMAN ARMY

2   FOR NEARLY forty-five years one problem obsessed
German military planners: how best to conduct a two-front
war against Russia and France. The first answer was a strong
army, and while Bismarck was weaving a cunning mesh of
European diplomacy his contemporary, the elder von Moltke,
was fashioning just such an instrument.[1]

Hero of Sedan and Chief of the German Great General
Staff from 1858–1888, Moltke originally envisaged an offensive
action against France, a fast, sharp attack to gain Germany a
separate peace and free her army for the eastern front against
Russia.

Moltke changed his mind in the years following when
France reorganized her army and fortified her eastern frontier.
Recognizing now that an attack against France would prove
costly, with no assurance of a decisive victory, Moltke saw
further that his own western frontier lent itself to defense.
Confident of his ability to hold it with meager forces, he
switched his offensive notions eastward.

Moltke's planning finally resulted in a defensive-offensive
strategy designed not to achieve total victory against either
Russia or France but sufficient victory to win Germany a

favorable peace.² To fight Russia Moltke planned a strong army
in East Prussia. Linked with other forces dispersed along the
450-mile border and with the Austrian army in Galicia, it
would defeat the Russian armies behind Kowno and Warsaw
while another German force, retreating if necessary to the
Rhine before fighting a "decisive battle," defended his western
border.

In 1888 Moltke bequeathed his policy to Count von Waldersee, the energetic and extremely ambitious officer who had
served as Quartermaster-General and Moltke's deputy since
1882. Influential in shaping Moltke's plans, Waldersee left
them just about as he found them, but his contribution to
Germany's future was considerable.

Waldersee's desire to fight a preventive war against Russia
collided squarely with Bismarck's diplomatic policy; the ensuing quarrel, in which Waldersee aligned himself with Baron
Holstein of the Foreign Office, ended, as we have seen, with
Bismarck's fall and General Caprivi's appointment. With
Caprivi's abandonment of the vital Reinsurance Treaty, and
Russia's subsequent alignment with France, the first link in
the ultimate chain of disaster was forged. Waldersee derived
a hollow victory. Not only did he anger the young Kaiser
Wilhelm II by arguing against his plans for a great navy but
he ran afoul of Caprivi by his constant attempts to subordinate
the War Ministry to the General Staff. He was dismissed in
1891.³

Waldersee's successor, Count Alfred von Schlieffen, is still
a controversial name in military history. Author of the so-
called Schlieffen plan, he has been damned as an impractical,
ruthless strategist who brought Germany and the world to
ruin; others have praised him as the most brilliant military
thinker since Napoleon.

Fifty-eight years old when he became Chief of the Great
General Staff, Schlieffen was a Prussian professional of thirty-
seven years' experience. He had entered the army after brief
study in law, served as a staff officer at Königgrätz and in the

Franco-Prussian War, and subsequently held a variety of important General Staff posts. Far the most influential event in his early life was the premature death of his wife Anna, after only four years of a happy marriage. Schlieffen was then thirty-six. Never a warm man, he grew more aloof and sarcastic, henceforth devoting his life solely to his profession with results even more unfortunate to his country than to himself.[4]

An adherent of Clausewitz and an admirer of Frederick the Great, Schlieffen found little to please him in the Moltke-Waldersee strategy. Defensive warfare, he soon concluded, led to protracted action, which was fatal to a country's economy; besides, it could never defeat the enemy and certainly not in the detail demanded by Clausewitz' definition of total victory.

Rather than a division of forces leading to what Moltke called "decisive victories" on both fronts and a favorable negotiated peace, Schlieffen wanted a concentration of force leading to swift, total victory on one front at a time. With this goal predominant he began a reappraisal of his operational heritage. Taking many years and nearly as many turns of mind, this resulted in his last official Memorandum of 1905— what often is called the Schlieffen plan.[5]

Under its terms the entire German army would deploy in the west unless Russia came into the war with France. In that event a force of ten divisions, selected equitably from the western armies, would be sent to East Prussia to hold the Russian offensive until Germany beat France—a matter of six weeks according to Schlieffen's estimate.

With an Italian army using Austrian and German railways to reach and defend the Upper Rhine area, Schlieffen planned to defend Alsace-Lorraine with two weak German armies comprising altogether five corps. This force would tie into the fortified bastion of Metz-Diedenhofen, which would serve further as a pivot for his right-wing offensive, an action given to five armies of some thirty-five corps stretching from Metz-Diedenhofen along the frontiers of Luxembourg, Belgium and

Holland. The extreme right wing of this offensive force would be composed of two very strong armies made up of sixteen corps and five cavalry divisions—the best Germany had.

To overcome the Belgian fortress of Liége, which lay in the path of the offensive, Schlieffen's extreme right-wing army would advance across the tip of Holland from where it could take Liége in flank from the north. Schlieffen hoped to overcome the moral censure that would result from violating neutral countries by a diplomatic agreement with Holland to permit the transit over her territory; more subtly, he hoped that his impressive concentrations along the Belgian-Dutch borders would suck France into defensive positions in Belgium, thus justifying his own invasion.[6]

Once the heavy right wing advanced, Schlieffen would reinforce it by two army corps from his left wing, situation permitting, and by six *Ersatz* divisions composed of surplus trained reserves. With this force protecting lines of communication, the right wing would debouch into northern France, sweep down west of Paris and wheel on the French armies, a gargantuan envelopment designed for swift, total victory.

Brilliant strategy here, but also some serious defects. In view of the 1905 political situation, the continued membership of Italy in the Triple Alliance was questionable. So, in view of the reluctant attitude of the *Reichstag* or German Parliament toward military expenditure, was the raising of the additional forces required. While Schlieffen appraised the enemy's offensive intentions remarkably well—he counted on a British force of 100,000 operating on the French left—he seems to have ignored the French Army's defensive capability, particularly the advantage it would gain by operating on interior lines, including a superb railway complex behind Paris. Although he built a magnificent railway system to effect his own rapid deployment within Germany, perhaps because he believed in a lightning victory in France Schlieffen paid scant attention to supplying his right wing by rail.

Schlieffen also paid little attention to external criticism, of which there was ample,[7] and refused to allow even healthy questioning by subordinates. But he did recognize some of the weak spots in his work and continued to treat them until his death in 1913. As his subsequent writings show, he was willing to consider minor adjustments in the plan, but to the end he believed in its essential strategy: crushing envelopment by successful exploitation of time-space factors. His deathbed words reportedly were, "It must come to a war. Keep the right wing strong."

Helmuth von Moltke, the fifty-eight-year-old nephew of the elder Moltke who replaced Schlieffen in 1906, possessed most of his predecessor's shortcomings and little of his imagination and boldness.[8] Moltke, with his splendid military appearance and aristocratic manners, had long been a favorite of Emperor Wilhelm II, who was said to find a comfortable tradition of victory in the name. According to Ludendorff the promotion "surprised everyone."[9] Though courteous to a marked degree and in some respects far above the intelligence of his colleagues, Moltke was scarcely the Prussian ideal: soft almost to the point of feyness, he embraced mysticism instead of mistresses, generally spent Staff journeys studying Goethe's *Faust* and writing soulful letters to his wife.[10]

Beset with doubts from the beginning of his appointment and soon fearful of the new spirit noted in the French Army, Moltke grew increasingly apprehensive over a major French offensive into Alsace-Lorraine. Unable to grasp Schlieffen's reasoning that a temporary sacrifice of territory here would not interfere with the right-wing offensive, Moltke chose to reinforce his left at the expense of his right.

Of nine new divisions formed by 1914, eight went to the two armies on the left, which meant that the five corps allotted by Schlieffen were increased to eight plus.[11] Further, Schlieffen's planned transfer of two corps from left to right was canceled; the six *Ersatz* divisions, composed of untried reserves, which Schlieffen had scheduled to guard the lines of communication on the right, were now diverted to back up the left.

Schlieffen's right wing was eight times stronger than his left. Moltke's right wing was only three times stronger and he eliminated its reinforcement by either active corps or *Ersatz* divisions.

Moltke's other major change stemmed from his desire to keep Holland a neutral "windpipe." Instead of advancing through the Maastricht Appendix he would "try to come to an agreement with Belgium" to cross her territory, perhaps by promising her "territorial acquisitions if she becomes our ally or at least remains passive."[12] If this failed, and Moltke seemed to think it would, then he would invade her and take Liége by a *coup de main*.

Paying more attention than had Schlieffen to technical developments, Moltke did contribute to the already high quality of the German Army. According to Ludendorff he worked hard to provide more heavy artillery and to give each artillery piece 1,200 rounds of ammunition, besides trying to increase the efficiency of the army "in [obtaining] anything from Scheer telescopes for the staff to . . . better entrenching tools for the infantry."[13] Schlieffen had let the Emperor turn the annual maneuver into a three-ringed circus; Moltke made it a serious training effort. Early in his tenure he approved new field regulations based on the lessons of the Boer and Russo-Japanese Wars, he equipped his regular army corps with aircraft, and he re-outfitted his army in the new field-gray uniform.

Yet he failed to remedy the most outstanding deficiencies bequeathed to him. In the years just prior to the war France was training over 80 per cent of her potential recruits compared to Germany's mere 52 per cent. Attempting to rectify this, Ludendorff as Moltke's staff officer ran into so much opposition that his chief, rather than backing him, transferred him as "inconvenient."[14]

No more than Schlieffen did Moltke worry about the French defensive capability or the threat of a British force in France. Neither was he concerned with his supply problem in

France—in 1914 the question of rail transport to his right wing remained as open as in 1905.

Despite these weaknesses, the German Army presented an impressive sight upon mobilization in 1914. Incomparably the best trained and equipped force in Europe, seven of its eight field armies or about 1,600,000 men were deployed on the western front.[15] A German army consisted of at least two infantry corps, nearly 90,000 troops, but could comprise seven corps plus auxiliary troops, as did Kluck's First Army which initially numbered over 300,000 men.

A German active corps numbered 44,000 troops—two infantry divisions plus such corps troops as *Jäger* or light infantry, cavalry, heavy artillery, signal, medical, engineer and supply and combat trains plus an air detachment of twelve planes. The reserve corps, of which Germany mobilized fourteen, possessed neither corps artillery nor aircraft, but their state of training was high enough to deploy them alongside active corps, one of the biggest surprises of the war.[16]

Numbering 17,500 men, a German active infantry division included two infantry and one artillery brigades plus small units, normally companies, of engineers, pioneers, medical and communication personnel. Artillery consisted of fifty-four 77-mm. guns and eighteen 105-mm. howitzers. Corps artillery added 105-mm. howitzers and 150-mm. howitzers, while army commanders could call for additional heavy guns including 210-mm. mortars and, for siege work, 420-mm. mortars, the largest yet developed in war.[17]

The advantage of this tremendous superiority in heavy artillery was offset by poor co-ordination between the infantry and artillery, poor use of air-directed artillery fire and by a poor-quality fuse that resulted in numerous duds. Although each gun carried some 1,200 rounds, each neatly packed in a handmade wicker basket, a prevailing doctrine of zone fire— the indiscriminate, very wasteful spraying of an entire area— further decreased artillery effectiveness.

Armed with 1898 Mauser clip-fed, bolt-action rifles and

dressed in field-gray uniforms, the German infantrymen stood well equipped in every item from waterproof cowhide packs to the famous spiked helmet that was light, cool and waterproof and shaded the eyes and back of the neck.[18] Backed by the 1908 water-cooled Maxim machine gun, the small unit was trained aggressively and so disciplined as to follow any order, but officers tempered primarily offensive tactics with an understanding of temporary emplacements including barbed wire and machine guns in the defense.

Besides twenty-two active and fourteen reserve infantry corps, the Germans deployed four cavalry corps, or a total ten divisions. A division of 7,000 men formed three cavalry brigades, three *Jäger* or light-infantry battalions, plus supporting units. Each brigade included a mounted machine-gun section of six guns and two batteries or a total of twelve 77-mm. guns of horse artillery. The troopers were trained and equipped to fight in close co-ordination with supporting *Jäger* battalions (partially bicycle-mounted), still another innovation. The cavalry suffered, however, from a lack of such equipment as entrenching tools, spades, climbing irons, wire cutters, tenting and horseshoes.[19]

In many respects the German soldiers were better equipped and trained than their French and British opposites, and they certainly were supported by a preponderance of machine guns and artillery. The attitude inculcated into the ranks is tersely offered by an excerpt from the 1912 edition of the Great General Staff handbook:

The general spirit of the German Army is one of intense devotion to Emperor and Fatherland, combined with the conviction that no other army in the world could stand up to them for any length of time. Owing to its numbers, its organization, its discipline, the absolute interrelation of its parts, the elaborateness and thoroughness of method which govern all its movements, and the strong spirit of the offensive inherent in the whole military hierarchy, there is no doubt that it is by far the most formidable fighting machine in the western world.[20]

This overconfidence resulting from belief rather than field experience was to prove perhaps the soldiers' greatest single defect, and one noted by a German military writer in 1912:

The German soldier, accustomed in times of peace to strict discipline, rigid attitudes and absolute obedience, is, in action, disconcerted by disorder, and thrown into confusion by the absence of his leaders. He has need in the hour of danger of the presence of an officer. Under the influence of his officers he will do anything that duty and discipline demand; he will follow his leader to certain death with calm and dignified enthusiasm, but left in a crowd he will quickly lose his head and forget what his education in time of peace will have taught him.[21]

Until 1914 war to the German had been a matter of neat field maneuvers with each soldier comfortably filling a slot, be it a general of division or the lowliest horse holder. When war became a matter of bullet and shell, of blood and casualties and disrupted communications, when junior officers suddenly had to act on their own initiative or when noncommissioned officers had to replace officers, the system tended to break down. Nor did the confusion of shooting war confine itself to the lower ranks.

On the eve of battle the officers commanding the impressive German armies presented striking contrasts among themselves in personality, ability and character, as did their French and British opposites. Not since Wellington's campaigns on the Spanish Peninsula or at Waterloo was the battlefield to witness such command eccentricities; as individual commanders in Wellington's day often unduly influenced a battle, so would these modern commanders shape the forthcoming conflict— some more than others, some with good results, some with bad.

Each of Moltke's seven army commanders held positive ideas as to the conduct of the impending campaign; each saw the decisive victory forming on his own front, no matter the expense to other fronts. Moltke's best commanders, Kluck and Bülow, were both sixty-eight years old, highly irascible professionals who had no use for Moltke. The Westphalian

Kluck did not like Bülow, a Prussian, and Bülow seems to have held both Kluck on his right and the Saxon Hausen on his left in contempt. Hausen, who resembled a British officer in appearance, was also dominated by the royal Duke Albrecht of Württemberg, commanding the Fourth Army on his left. German Crown Prince Wilhelm, commanding the Fifth Army, had to answer to no one (except his father), and nearly as untouchable was Crown Prince Rupprecht of Bavaria, commanding the Sixth Army and dominating von Heeringen, a former Minister of War who commanded the Seventh Army on the extreme left. Able, usually ambitious General Staff officers such as Krafft von Dellmensingen served the royal army commanders as professional chiefs of staff, nor did they hesitate to use royal prerogatives to get their way.

Here was a group of prima donnas which probably would have produced effectively if someone had cracked a brisk enough whip. But by 1914 illness combined with natural reticence had removed what slight resemblance Helmuth von Moltke ever bore to a proper commander.[22] Worse yet, following the example of his famous uncle he saw his task restricted to training and planning for war; with the armies assembled and ordered to march, the commander was to remain in the background, his will being imposed by the army commanders.

This was all right except that it presupposed a commander who had attained a strategic unity with his subordinates before the war began, and one who if matters went wrong would intervene decisively to set them right. Moltke had not accomplished the first by 1914, and was incapable of accomplishing the second. Caught at the outbreak of war taking a cure at Karlsbad, the sick old man returned to Berlin where General Staff headquarters now became the Supreme Command—the *Oberste Heeresleitung* or OHL. There, miles from the armies, he fed himself on what reports were given out by his deputy, General von Stein—reports prepared by his major staff officers, von Tappen of Operations, von Dommes and Hentsch of Intelligence. These three lieutenant colonels, bright enough

General Staff officers, were hardly senior or capable enough to give OHL the commanding voice it lacked. Still, such was the inviolate code of the Great General Staff that when these young OHL officers did visit army commands they spoke with the authority of Moltke—a curious system that, as will be seen, added to the confusion resulting from lack of top leadership.

And lack of top leadership was the chief deficiency of the German Army at the beginning of World War I. That it was to win impressive initial victories without Moltke's leadership is not surprising. It was a strong army, well trained and equipped—fairly bursting with martial *élan*. But not the least factor in its success was due to an outside source. This was the enemy, France, and the very inept plans of her General Staff.

# A CAMPAIGN OF ROPES

3     A DEFENSIVE POWER always suffers tactically vis-à-vis an aggressor who retains the initiative. An objective assessment of the aggressor's capabilities is the basis of any defense and was so in France in the years before the war. Not believing that Germany could mount sufficient strength for such a wide sweep as that threatened by the Schlieffen plan, and hampered by Belgian neutrality, British caution, and domestic political dissension, the French General Staff worked out a number of plans that culminated in the famous—or infamous—Plan XVII.

Plan XVII evolved with no more ease but in a considerably different manner from Germany's final war plans. The Franco-Prussian War left France a defeated nation with a shattered and humiliated army confined to purely defensive thought.

For fifteen years after the Peace of Frankfurt, General Miribel dominated the French Army with a doctrine of passive defense rather than offense, while the great engineer General Séré de Rivière rebuilt a frontier left naked by German seizure of Alsace-Lorraine, including the key French fortress of Metz.[1] Rivière's expensive program resulted in a line of fortifications linked by the bastions of Belfort–Epinal–Toul–Verdun, a fixed defense solely designed to shield the slow-moving French Army against a German attack until it could deploy in defensive positions northeast of Paris.[2]

Two developments altered this defensive strategy. In 1885 new high-explosive artillery shells rendered Rivière's forts more susceptible to assault. A viable defense of the nearly 200-mile eastern border now meant a more rapid concentration of armies further forward, a capability now within reach due to long overdue improvements in the eastern railway system.

General Miribel's Plan VIII of 1887 changed French strategy from the purely defensive to the defensive-offensive, a situation that lasted until a few years before the war. Plan VIII envisaged a German attack confined to certain gaps along the fortified border, especially through the forty-mile-wide Trouée de Charmes between Toul and Epinal. Positioned behind these gaps to take such canalized attacks in the flank, French armies then would turn the German offensive into a French victory in Alsace-Lorraine by a sharp counterattack.

The French Army's growth to its next important transition is much too involved for these pages, but a few events must be mentioned. Political and military dissension ruled the years: General Boulanger's abortive *coup d'état* led to the anti-Semitic Dreyfus case that divided France into two armed camps, with enormous harm to the Army. The related anticlerical crusades of General André followed to split further Army and nation.

But during these years the intellectual élite of the Army began hearing Cardot's lectures on Clausewitz' offensive doctrines and began reading and believing du Picq's famous teachings on the value of moral will in battle.[3] Spearheaded by General Langlois and younger officers such as Foch, Lanrezac, Castelnau, Bourderiat and Grandmaison, the new school weathered the political storms while fighting extremist factions that sprang up in competition, the most important being General de Negrier's doctrine of extreme defense.[4]

The new school did not gain immediate popularity. But by emphasizing the offensive as the proper instrument to avenge humiliating defeat its teachings contained the appeal of rebellion against traditional defeatism and won it lasting and important adherents throughout the army and in political circles.[5] Its radical arguments were buttressed by the increased improvement in the French railway system, by development of the rapid-fire 75-mm. field gun—a fantastic advance in artillery[6]— and by the changing political situation which strengthened the alliance with Russia, brought England into an *Entente Cordiale* and made Italy's continued loyalty to the Triple Alliance doubtful.

In 1909 General de Lacroix issued the last traditional plan of the French high command, Plan XVI. Wedded to General Miribel's defensive-offensive strategy of yesteryear, Plan XVI concentrated the bulk of the French Army in considerable depth behind Epinal and Verdun, with covering cavalry forces on the left as far as Rethel and covering armies on the right behind Belfort and the Alps. Predicated on a major German attack through Lorraine, this plan envisaged a defense for a month, or long enough for Russia to mobilize against Germany in the east. Once Russia took the offensive, the French mass of maneuver south of the line Metz–Paris would be brought up to the counterattack which, in concert with a British army on the left, would be followed by a counteroffensive into Alsace-Lorraine.

This plan lasted until 1911, when General Michel, who as vice-president of the Supreme War Council (*Conseil Supérieur de la Guerre*) was commander-in-chief designate in time of war, submitted a new plan based on an assumption that Germany would violate Belgium in a wide attack west of the Meuse.[7] Michel proposed to meet such an attack by shifting his major force to the left at the expense of the Lorraine front, which he would defend with minor forces. To gain troop increases for his greatly extended front he proposed to augment regular army units with reserve units, a scheme that would raise each active regiment to a "demi-brigade" and one similar to that already being put into effect in Germany.[8]

Despite Michel's accurate prognostication of German intentions, his new plan presented several difficulties. By concentrating his force on the left, effective action would mean
violating Belgian neutrality and thus sacrificing British aid.
To meld reserves with regulars assumed a combat readiness
of reserves not warranted by fact and it also ignored the vola-
tile political question of calling up reserves short of war. More
important, the plan involved an initial sacrifice of French
territory west of Alsace-Lorraine.

Even before the Council debated it, Michel's plan brought
down the wrath of the offensive school, which used it to
launch the long-brewing rebellion. In two brilliant and force-
ful lectures at the new Center of Higher War Studies, Lieutenant Colonel de Grandmaison, Chief of Operations in the
War Ministry, threw the doctrine of the *offensive à outrance*
in as a challenge to the still prevalent tradition of the defensive-
offensive.

Under Grandmaison's terms war could not be fought by
defensive actions; instead, aggressive spirit won wars. "For
the attack only two things are necessary: to know where the
enemy is and to decide what to do. What the enemy intends
to do is of no consequence."[9] Every traditional consideration governing tactics must be subordinated to the spirit of
the offense—terrain, security, supporting forces, artillery preparation, each became unimportant, indeed disastrous, if allowed to inhibit the infantry assault. Spirit and spirit alone ruled:
"imprudence became a virtue."[10]

Taken along with Michel's plan, the then raging Moroccan
crisis and omnipresent Gallic temperament, Grandmaison's
lectures raised a storm so turbulent that three Ministers of
War rose and fell between February and July of 1911. The
bubbling pot boiled over at a meeting of the Supreme War
Council on July 19. At Michel's insistence his army reorganization plan, though not his new plan of operations, was placed
on the agenda by Messimy, his enemy, who was perennially
being reappointed Minister of War. After violently criticiz-

ing the plan the generals unanimously voted it down. Michel was finished; Messimy dismissed him two days later.

Messimy offered Michel's post to Galliéni, the doughty old pacifier-governor of Madagascar, who turned it down on the grounds he had been instrumental in Michel's fall and could not personally profit from it. Galliéni recommended General Pau, whose condition that he have full control in appointing general officers made him unacceptable. Messimy next turned to a rather junior general, Joseph Jacques Césaire Joffre, who with Pau's blessing accepted.

One of eleven children of a poor Pyrenees family, at fifty-nine Joffre was a veteran of the Franco-Pussian War and of long colonial service, part of it under Galliéni. He was known as a very capable engineer and a resolute soldier who had proved himself in several campaigns—in Timbuktu, when the Touareg natives cut up General Bonnier's expeditionary force, Joffre took command and carried out the pacification of the territory, an act that won him the coveted Legion of Honor and promotion to lieutenant colonel.[11]

Joffre wore his dress as simply as his manner, and both bordered on a quiet rudeness that could change to immense charm enhanced by an earthy sense of humor. Later, in the midst of crisis, he would be asked what he thought of the Scot kilt and would reply with that typical Gallic shrug of contempt, "*Pour l' amour, magnifique. Pour le guerre, p—— l——.*" Later, too, his personal qualities would combine into a monument of will and determination perhaps unique in the history of war. But now, to the French Army of 1911, he was a taciturn professional who had commanded a division and corps with distinction and, important to politicians, was a republican who had avoided personal intrigue during the difficult purge years. No intellectual giant, Joffre nevertheless possessed a common sense embodying flexibility of action. Militarily he aligned himself with the offensive school, but not to the extent of its most vociferous adherents.

Joffre's appointment was a popular one, which fact Messimy used, with the imminent danger of war with Germany over Morocco, to push through a partial reorganization of the high command. Joffre soon received the new title, Chief of the General Staff, and with it some control over the formerly independent general staff.[12]

With General Castelnau his first assistant and Major Gamelin his *Chef de Cabinet* or Staff Secretary, Joffre wasted little time in consolidating his office and turning to a strategic reappraisal of both Plan XVI and Michel's plan, which he found in his safe. Dissatisfied with both, he worked out an interim plan called "Variation Number One" which shifted his front north to Mezières and moved his mass of maneuver further forward. While working this out he sent General Dubail to Russia to impress the Czar with the need for rapid offensive action on the eastern front in case of war with Germany. Fully co-operative, the Czar agreed to act before completing mobilization and to cross the Prussian frontier on the sixteenth day of war with two armies. "It is at the very heart of Germany that we must strike," he told Dubail. "The objective of both of us ought to be Berlin."[13]

Such words fell warmly on Joffre's ears, for even then he was preparing a new doctrine of warfare, a complex task undertaken at his direction by members of the Supreme War Council and their staffs, and by members of the General Staff, the War College and the Center of Higher War Studies.

Their finished products leave no doubt as to the overwhelming influence of the doctrinal *offensive à outrance*. *Regulations for the Conduct of Large Units*, published in October, 1913, as a guide to principal commanders, stressed that "success in war could come only to him who sought to bring the opponent to battle and was capable of delivering it offensively with all his power." Equally aggressive were *Regulations for Armies in the Field*, published in December, 1913, and given to division and lower unit commanders, and the *Infantry Regulations*, published in April, 1914, for the troops and still being studied when war began.

With this effort under way Joffre's attention turned to strategy. At the very beginning of his tenure he ran afoul of the nebulous position occupied by Belgium vis-à-vis the French border. Militarily he wanted to use the little country in his opening offensive. To Joffre a move through Luxembourg and Belgium which would avoid the strongly fortified German position of Metz–Thionville and corridored, very limited fronts in the Lorraine country held all of the appeal that it did to Schlieffen, though Joffre envisaged no such wide sweep. Convinced that the Germans would violate Belgian neutrality if it suited their purposes, Joffre soon after his appointment explained to his government the purely military value of violating Belgian neutrality first, then asked if such could be considered.

Although President Poincaré held no qualms about violating the Grand Duchy of Luxembourg, which he rightly considered Germany's pawn, and although he even hedged when it came to respecting Belgian neutrality, the political facts were obvious: Belgium's position stemmed from the Treaty of 1839 which England (and Russia and Germany) had signed. If France deliberately invaded her, no matter the military justification, then France could expect to forfeit England's aid. So conscious was England of the value of world opinion that in 1906 Lieutenant Colonel Repington of the British General Staff (later military correspondent of the *Times*) warned the French, "Do not let yourselves be tempted to enter Belgium upon a simple threat from Germany; it might be in the interest of that country to push you towards such a step"—a timely warning in view of Schlieffen's reasoning discussed earlier.[14]

Had the joint military talks authorized by England's Secretary of State for War, Mr. Haldane, come to nought, as they seemed to do until 1910, France might not have worried so much about the sensitivity of her new ally. But under the impetus of the Francophile Brigadier General Henry Wilson, Director of Military Operations in the War Office from 1910 on, they prospered. After the Moroccan crisis of 1911 England's once tentative suggestion of aid became a very real, if unwritten, promise: staff talks even then were based on a British Expeditionary Force[15] of "six infantry divisions, one cavalry division and two mounted brigades, a total of 125,000 men" which would be ready to start military operations in France "on the fifteenth day of mobilization."[16]

Although Repington's 1906 warning was repeated to the French by Lord Esher in 1911,[17] Britain's commitment to France now made it desirable for her to renew an understanding with Belgium. British diplomats and military officers tried unsuccessfully in 1912; in November, with Sir Edward Grey's authority, Henry Wilson told the French General Staff

that Belgium was hesitating as to the attitude she would take in the case of war between France and Germany, and that she seemed to incline rather to the German side. Now if France should be the first to violate Belgian neutrality, the army of Belgium would certainly join the Germans and the British Government would then be called upon to defend the neutrality of that country. This would place us in a very embarrassing position; therefore, the French Army has no interest whatever in being the first to violate Belgian neutrality.[18]

These words sounded the death knell to Joffre's hopes for elastic strategy but in no way deterred him from his offensive course. Convinced that to win the war he must "seize the initiative" and "assemble every available man for battle" he persuaded the government to pass the famous "cadre" laws which streamlined the basic organization of infantry, artillery and cavalry; in reply to German troop increases near the frontier he asked that the two-year recruiting law of 1905 be changed to a three-year law.

During the ensuing debates Joffre in late 1912 worked out "Variation Number Two" to Plan XVI and followed it in May, 1913, with the Plan XVII that controlled the concentration of French and British armies when war broke out in 1914.

Under its terms the bulk of French force was divided into five field armies supported by a cavalry corps, two groups of reserve divisions and groups of heavy and mobile heavy artillery. Greatly strengthened covering forces would fight a defensive action along the northeastern frontier until the thirteenth day of mobilization. Then the two right-wing armies, the First and Second, would attack into Lorraine, the center or Third Army would attack east of Metz, and the left or Fifth Army, positioned opposite the Ardennes, would attack either into Belgium or straight ahead toward Metz, depending on the route of the German invasion. The final or Fourth Army was held in reserve left of center. Reserve divisions buttressed either flank and a cavalry corps would operate on the Fifth Army's left as contact with the BEF still further left.

Unlike the Schlieffen plan as modified by Moltke, which dictated an entire operation, Plan XVII was essentially a plan of concentration so developed that the commander-in-chief could "advance with all forces united to the attack of the German armies."[19] In essence it was nothing so much as a refined *compression* of earlier French plans. The increased strength of the Russian Army, its willingness to assume an early offensive in the east, the British commitment to send an army to France, the nearly certain fact of Italian neutrality— each lent itself to the resurgence of French spirit, a pervasive governing attitude that offered Joffre the increased means to what all thought would be a swift and victorious military end.

To accomplish that end in 1914 Joffre commanded an army considerably less impressive though larger in numbers than the German Army. Upon mobilization 5 field armies plus reserve divisions and artillery groups numbered about 1,650,000 troops. Due to fight on its left were another 100,000 troops of the BEF's 2 infantry corps and a cavalry division. Belgium was mobilizing an army of 175,000, but little could be expected either from its 1 cavalry or 6 infantry divisions, which were poorly trained and equipped.

Similar in structure to the German corps, each of the 21 French active infantry corps counted 40,000 men; they lacked heavy artillery but carried more field guns. Each corps maintained a reserve brigade of 2 infantry regiments as part of corps troops. But the French—unlike the Germans—did not integrate their 25 reserve divisions into the field armies, and at first preferred to fight their 10 cavalry divisions as independent units rather than in corps formation.[20]

The French active division, numbering about 15,000, was nearly equal in machine-gun strength to the German; the British division, some 18,000 strong, carried the same complement of machine guns as the enemy and also excellent heavy artillery.[21] Although the French were in bad shape when it came to heavy artillery, in field guns neither the German 77-mm. gun nor the British 13-pdr. could compare in numbers or performance with the French 75-mm. gun, which was deadly accurate and fired twice as fast as the others.[22] French artillery training was excellent, particularly in the use of cover and concealment; a common phrase of artillery commanders was, "*Une batterie vue est une batterie perdue.*"[23]

Carrying a muzzle-loading 1886 Lebel rifle and wearing red trousers topped by a long, clumsy combination jacket-cloak of blue—the "*capote*"—and loaded with poncho, pack, entrenching tool, bulky mess gear, a cooking pot and an extra pair of hobnail boots, the French infantryman presented a picture at odds with the swift charges demanded by the *offensive à outrance*. Yet, very significantly and unlike the German, he marched with fixed bayonet, a deadly-looking, thin, triangular piece of needle steel vital to the favorite order of his officer, "*A la baionnette! En avant!*" The British Tommy, falling neatly between the two, carried the excellent if heavy Lee-Enfield clip-fed, bolt-action rifle, wore a light khaki uniform ideal except for winter war, and was trained for offense and defense—equipment and training both having resulted from experience gained in the Boer War. Much more individualistic in outlook than the German or Frenchman, he had been taught and partially understood the importance of fast, accurate rifle fire, of advance by fire and movement, and of cover and concealment.

French cavalry suffered, comparatively, in everything from doctrine to equipment. Dressed in steel breastplates and polished helmets with horsehair plumes, the French cuirassiers and dragoons carried lances and an obsolete 1892 Lebel carbine, the *"mosqueton."* Ill equipped for dismounted fighting, the cavalryman rode his horse well, treated it badly.[24] Though lacking accompanying infantry such as the German *Jäger* units, British cavalrymen were trained for both mounted and dismounted fighting and carried rifles instead of the usual light carbines. The British cavalry always maintained that its rifle shooting was every bit as good as that of the infantry, and this training extended to all the ancillary personnel in a cavalry regiment.[25] In addition, the single massive cavalry division sent out with the BEF—14,000 troops disposed in 5 brigades—was armed with light machine guns and horse artillery.

To the steady, almost phlegmatic British soldier and the eager, overconfident German, the French *poilu* stood in amazing contrast. Lacking the unity of purpose that bound together the German legions, the French units might have been disastrously infected by the discord arising from the turbulent politics of the previous half-century, in which a man had to be categorized as cleric, anticleric, freethinker, monarchist, socialist, traditionalist, antimilitarist, Catholic, Protestant or Jew. The professional Army, however, at least in the ranks, seemed singularly free from discord—perhaps one result of the fire infused by Grandmaison's offensive renascence. As for the reservists, love of country combined with hatred of the enemy surmounted personal attitudes. Such was the hurly-burly quality of the first weeks and months of war that private feelings were not plentifully recorded, but enough survived to show the evident cohesiveness of that air. Let some letters speak:

*Pierre Génin, avowed antimilitarist:* I leave with courage in the hope that our loyalty and possibly our sacrifice will benefit our children. They must live in the enjoyment of that peace of which we have dreamed. If our youth, if our strength, may serve to establish their man's existence, we shall then have fought for our ideal which remains a living and a happy fact beyond this lightning and this thunder. In this upheaval our vision shall not be dulled. And now, off with a quick step and a keen eye to smash these savages!

*François Baudry, a twenty-four-year-old scientist:* If I die, it will be as a good Frenchman, a good Catholic, and a good Vendéan [a resident of the Vendée province]. . . . Feeling absolutely calm, I hope with the grace of God to set the example I owe to my grade as an officer, to my position in society, and to my being the great-grandson of the *Géants du Bocage.*

*Albert Thierry, trade-union professor and radical:* August 12, 1914. I leave in a quarter of an hour, 28th Infantry, 26th Company, Evreux. . . . If we are to be vanquished, it would mean that justice does not exist, and to live in a world devoid of justice would hardly seem worth while. . . .

*Jacques de Laumont, a youngster writing to his mother:* With all my heart I will fight for France and for you. I will be brave, you will see.[26]

Such spirit was not so obvious in the high command. Like their German opposites most of the French commanders were old, all were temperamental. Lanrezac commanded the Fifth Army; born in Guadeloupe, he was a swarthy old military academician who hated the British and was going to fight alongside them. Galliéni, like Joffre born in the Pyrenees, was very old, ill and in retirement; a good soldier and politically a powerful one, he had been selected by Joffre to replace him as commander-in-chief in an emergency. Pau, who left an arm on the 1870 battlefield, was also in retirement; too old, he was recalled anyway and given command of the extreme right. Langle, commanding the Fourth Army, was still another called from retirement, but one who refused to be beaten when it came to the test. Castelnau commanded the Second Army; a Catholic like Foch serving under him, "the fighting friar"—as the army called him—was short and broad, his face covered with imperial-style whiskers as aristocratic as his demeanor. All this was a splendid contrast to Dubail, commanding the First Army on his right, a tall, slender, solemn officer whose deep-set eyes caused his face to resemble that of a worried spaniel.

Commanding under these top generals from corps to brigade level were a fearful lot of noneffectives, but also some excellent officers destined to make their marks: the dashing Franchet d'Esperey; the aggressive Maud'huy; the hard-charging little Ferdinand Foch, already famous as a military writer-teacher; the aloof Pétain, now only a fifty-eight-year-old colonel commanding a brigade.

Joffre would have trouble, lots of it, with some of these officers, nor would his problems lessen with the arrival of the BEF whose commander, Field Marshal Sir John French, was then putting together a staff at the Hotel Metropole in London.

But unlike Moltke, the French commander-in-chief stood ready for trouble or for any of the other vicissitudes brought on by the job of command. Believing in the Napoleonic concept of centralized command, the sixty-two-year-old Joffre held every intention of influencing the action as it developed. Though a generation removed in time and a world removed in manner from Wellington, the prosaic Joffre agreed with the Iron Duke's famous dictum:

[The French marshals] planned their campaigns just as you might make a splendid set of harness. It looks very well, and answers very well until it gets broken; and then you are done for. Now, I made my campaign of ropes. If anything went wrong, I tied a knot and went on.[27]

Joffre was going to have to "tie knots" because the shortcomings of Plan XVII soon would loom large. But despite its errors, resulting from false estimates of enemy intentions and strength and overconfidence in French capabilities, it contained one immense saving grace. By compressing but not deserting the fundamental tenet of the defensive-offensive strategy, by forming a campaign of ropes, Plan XVII left the initiative of decision to a commander who was willing to change his mind before time ran out.

# CONFUSION AND
# *CHENILLES*

4    THE SUCCESS of the German offensive rested on a *coup de main* against Liége, the Belgian city-fortress which the enemy hoped to capture within forty-eight hours.

Von Emmich, commanding the X Corps in Bülow's Second Army, won the task: spearheaded by cavalry, Emmich's special striking force of six reinforced brigades crossed into Belgium on August 4, brushed aside cursory resistance and by morning finished an eighteen-mile march over torn-up roads to approach the target.

No easy nut to crack, Liége rose from either side of the Meuse River, encircled by a dozen reinforced concrete forts firing some 400 guns and defended by about 40,000 soldiers including a newly arrived division and brigade. A vigorous old veteran named General Leman commanded this garrison, and he intended to carry out his personal orders from King Albert "to hold to the end."[1]

Early on August 5 Leman brusquely refused a demand to surrender and Emmich opened an artillery bombardment. Infantry assaults in the afternoon and evening ran into determined and unexpected resistance, and failed despite casualties so severe that Emmich had to call on Bülow for reinforcements.

Leman's mobile troops continued to hold their own on August 6, but now the weight of the German attacks coupled with new German cavalry penetrations from the north brought home to the Belgian commander the ultimate hopelessness of his situation: to save what he could he ordered his division and brigade to march to the rest of the army defending behind the Gette River.

This order helped bring fame to Erich von Ludendorff. Deputy Chief of Staff to Bülow, Ludendorff had accompanied Emmich's striking force as an observer. When General Wussow, commanding the 14th Brigade, was killed Ludendorff persuaded Emmich to give him the command. That night he personally led his troops to the inner citadel of Liége; it was now undefended by regular troops but his was nonetheless a brave action, resulting in occupation of the citadel and in capture of the city the next day.[2]

Although Emmich's excited message to Bülow on August 7 contained the cautionary statement, "As yet not known which forts have been taken," Bülow instead of waiting for details announced a "great victory" and displaced his headquarters forward from Hanover to Montjoie.[3] The next day he learned the ugly truth: the ring of forts remained unbroken, with General Leman's headquarters transferred to Fort Roncin, and Emmich and the 14th Brigade were cut off in the city they had captured!

Desperately Bülow threw in remaining elements of several corps under von Einem, who succeeded in establishing communication with Emmich but not in rescuing him. Emmich finally freed himself on August 10 by capturing Fort Barchon from the rear. With that Einem's force captured the neighboring fort, thus clearing the way for heavy siege artillery, immense 420-mm. guns that blasted the first tactical surprise of the war. One after the other the Belgian forts, built to withstand 210-mm. fire, crumbled. Late on August 15 General Leman was carried unconscious from Fort Roncin. The last forts struck their colors the next day.

Before the first German cannon fired on Liége Moltke's confidence had been shaken by the Kaiser. In the forlorn hope of gaining British neutrality, Wilhelm ingenuously ordered Moltke to march his army east against Russia. Utterly amazed Moltke explained that this was technically impossible. "Your uncle would have given me a different answer," the Emperor said.

According to Moltke, "I felt as if my heart would break . . . when I got home I was like a broken man, and shed tears of despair. . . ." Events quickly terminated the crisis, but Moltke was unable "to get over this experience. It was as though something in me had been irretrievably shaken. My confidence and self-reliance were destroyed."[4]

The inauspicious opening of the war at Liége did nothing to rebuild them, but soon more favorable reports began arriving in OHL headquarters, still located in the General Staff building hard by the Brandenburg Gate in Berlin. Mobilization and concentration plans developed with incredible smoothness: beginning on August 6 550 trains a day crossed the Rhine, an effort that brought a million and a half troops to forward zones by August 12.

Too, on August 9 Heeringen on the left reported a victory in Alsace. By August 12 the First Army's cavalry on the right was prowling around the Belgian main line of resistance on the Gette River; by August 15 Rupprecht was reporting a new French offensive into Lorraine, an unexpected though welcome move greeted with initial delaying actions; and by August 16 when Liége fell, the Second Army's cavalry was probing the French defenses at Dinant.

Compared to overall progress by August 16, Moltke's difficulties were few. Admittedly he had committed his six *Ersatz* divisions to beef up his left, but this didn't bother him. No more did he worry about the location of the British army; some time earlier he had told Admiral Tirpitz, who volunteered to contest the naval movement of the BEF, "that this was not necessary, and it would even be of advantage if the

Armies of the West could settle with the 160,000 English at the same time as the French and Belgians."[5]

Perhaps Moltke's attitude would have changed had he realized how inaccurately the French were estimating his own strength and intentions. But even without that, he should have felt pleased with his general situation when on August 17 he moved his headquarters to Coblenz and ordered the advance of his great right wing.

Instead, his doubts fed upon themselves, his apprehensions continued to grow. Helmuth von Moltke was a nervous man.

The same day Emmich began his assault at Liége, General Joseph Joffre arrived at his secret field headquarters—the *Grand Quartier Général* or GQG—at Vitry-le-François, a quiet little town on the Marne about seventy miles west from Castelnau's Second Army at Nancy. There, under the aegis of the dapper General Belin, assisted by the genial 240-pound General Berthelot, he found his large staff occupying an old schoolhouse. Working eight-hour shifts around the clock, brisk young General Staff officers were handling the details involved in some 4,000 train movements besides processing the reports beginning to come in from the front.[6]

Plan XVII called for a less dramatic opening of the war than the German action. Joffre's planned offensive in Lorraine —a move motivated as much by a political desire to reclaim the lost provinces of Alsace and Lorraine as by military necessity—could not begin until August 14 when mobilization and concentrations were complete and when the first Russian army had begun to move, nor could any offensive on the left be supported until the British arrived. Essential to either offensive was an accurate estimate of the enemy build-up and direction of attack, a process hindered from the beginning by preconceived beliefs and by contradictory information flowing in from a disorganized Belgian Army.

GQG's *bête-noir* stemmed from the completely mistaken but enduring belief that German reserve corps and divisions were employed behind and separate from their regular forces—the conventional method, which Germany had dropped years before. This erroneous assumption automatically gave the lie to a good many accurate indications of German concentrations received in these opening days. It created not only a false picture of German strength along the entire battle line, but particularly of the German right—the beginning of a disastrous error that precluded thought of a wide German right-wing sweep around the French left.

This danger was suggested in part to Joffre by his Fifth Army commander, General Lanrezac, on July 31, next on August 8 by Lanrezac's chief of staff, Hely d'Oissel. Joffre gave their pessimism short shrift: they and he lacked any indications of such a move, indeed reports from Liége stressed the disorganized nature of German attacks, the demoralized attitude of German prisoners. Moreover Sordet's cavalry corps was screening Lanrezac's left and patrolling in Belgium, and Joffre was reinforcing the Fifth Army with two divisions newly arrived from Africa.[7]

In truth Joffre, and he was not alone, had converted the negative information received from Belgium into a positive conclusion made the more dangerous by traditional belief that the major German concentration was forming around Metz–Thionville. With his left safe and his center building, the way lay open for an offensive from his right and this had begun by the time of d'Oissel's visit to GQG on August 8.

On August 7 General Bonneau's reinforced VII Corps of Dubail's First Army had pushed across the Alsatian border toward Colmar, a preliminary move designed to anchor the French right firmly on the Rhine and to win the psychological victory inherent in occupying the former French province. Not imbued with Grandmaison's teachings, Bonneau crawled; by nightfall he had advanced but three miles into German territory nor did he gain his first objective, the village of Mülhausen, until the following afternoon. There he reported the extreme fatigue of his troops—and halted. The next morning advance units of Heeringen's Seventh Army fell on his lines, captured 300 of his soldiers and sent him in panic-stricken retreat back to the Belfort fortifications.

The disaster created a storm in French official circles: even before Bonneau reached Belfort Minister of War Messimy notified Joffre that "the Government demands that any general officer who does not perform his duty with the requisite firmness shall be brought before a general court-martial and shot within twenty-four hours." Joffre sensibly interpreted the order as giving him authority to relieve Bonneau and his subordinates of their commands, the first of a long series of such actions.[8]

While Bonneau had been struggling toward Mülhausen, Joffre on August 8 issued General Instructions Number One, the document that underwrote the opening battles later to be known as the Battle of the Frontiers.[9] These orders called for two separate offensives, in reality the advance of his entire army. With his right reorganized into the Army of Alsace under the one-armed General Pau, Joffre ordered Dubail's First Army and Castelnau's Second Army to strike into Lorraine, a movement to be followed by his center and left armies attacking toward Thionville.

The First and Second Armies, a total of seven corps plus reserve divisions, artillery and cavalry—in all nearly a third of Joffre's strength—moved out on August 14. Successful skirmishes along the line, including a fight at Drespach which cost the Germans 2,000 casualties, offered the invaders first blood, the more enthusiastically tasted as they crossed the border and advanced into German territory.[10]

The first flaw developed on the right: delayed by reorganizing his new Army of Alsace, Pau failed to keep the pace. Too old and too cautious for the *offensive à outrance*, Pau soon turned into a latter-day Don Quixote halting to tilt at the puny windmills offered by a few German *Landwehr* units, a wasted effort that forced Dubail to shed a corps to screen his flank.

But if Pau erred on the side of caution Dubail and Castelnau ran away with optimism only too agreeable to Joffre back in GQG. The early successes of the French commanders against what they reported as "strong rear-guard forces" coincided nicely with Joffre's belief that these were outposts of a mere three plus German corps, a force that his two armies would soon annihilate.

By August 19 his optimism seemed justified by progress: Foch's XX Corps on the left faced the heights of Morhange, in the center Espinasse's XV Corps occupied Dieuze, and on the right de Castelli's VIII Corps held Sarrebourg on the main line of railroad connecting Strasbourg and Metz. Although Dubail's right flank was still weak from Pau's failure to advance, and the general frontal movement had been checked by increasing resistance in this difficult terrain of woods and lakes, both armies maintained an offensive posture. The aristocratic Castelnau, the fiery Dubail, the stolid Joffre—all were confident.

Moltke learned of the invasion on August 15. Tempted to throw Prince Wilhelm's Fifth Army at Metz against Castelnau's flank, he decided that it was too early to upset his general plan. He already had subordinated Heeringen's Seventh Army to Rupprecht, and now he reinforced the Sixth Army with a division from Metz and with his six *Ersatz* divisions.

Rupprecht, or more properly Krafft von Dellmensingen, his chief of staff, next moved three of Heeringen's corps to the right to meet Dubail's advance, a transfer causing him to postpone his planned counterattack, grudgingly approved by OHL, until August 20.[11] Meanwhile the German leaders in their headquarters at St. Avold let the French advance. German strength, estimated by GQG at three plus corps, actually amounted to nine infantry corps, a cavalry corps and six *Ersatz* divisions. The Germans knew every inch of the Lorraine country. They sat back—waiting.

Blissfully unaware of the hornet's nest on his right Joffre meanwhile concentrated on his center and left. On August 14 he revealed his thinking when General Lanrezac once again turned up to introduce the unpleasant subject of the French left. Joffre had just broken off a conversation with General Galliéni, sent by Minister of War Messimy to discuss GQG strategy—a subject Joffre always believed was his business alone—and was in no mood to heed Lanrezac's heatedly pressed arguments as to German right-wing intentions. Information from Belgium was still either negative or so contradictory as to defy reason, nor had Sordet accomplished anything in his reconnaissances except to tire out his horses.

Joffre did have to credit confirmed reports of German cavalry actions north of the Meuse, and on the following day he formed three reserve divisions on his extreme left into a group under General d'Amade, whom he ordered to establish a defensive line between Maubeuge and the sea.

But events that afternoon suddenly bore out Lanrezac's warning. German cavalry in force struck the Dinant bridges, an attack repulsed by d'Esperey's I Corps at the cost of about a thousand French casualties. Joffre now authorized Lanrezac to move the left wing of his Fifth Army into the triangle formed by the Sambre and Meuse Rivers behind the fortified Belgian city of Namur. If the Germans attacked north of Dinant across the Meuse they would be caught between Lanrezac's force, Namur and the Belgian Army on the left.

On August 16 Joffre explained his confident reasoning to Field Marshal Sir John French, whose British force was to fight on the left of Lanrezac's Fifth Army.[12] But even as the two old generals sat talking in Joffre's headquarters, the last fort at Liége pulled down its flag to clear the way for the German advance across Belgium.

England's late start in the war stemmed from Sir Edward Grey's genuine desire to preserve the peace of Europe coupled with his country's popular reluctance to fight unless Belgium were violated. As a result England did not declare war against

Germany until the night of August 4—when Emmich's brigades were marching on Liége.

Despite pre-war military talks with France, the British Government had never committed itself to an immediate plan of operations, a subject now taken up on August 5 when Prime Minister Asquith, acting also as Secretary of State for War, hastily convened a council of war at 10 Downing Street. Besides most of the Cabinet including Grey and Winston Churchill, such military notables as Lord Kitchener of Khartoum, who that day would be appointed Secretary of State for War, old Lord Roberts and Sir John French were on hand to decide what military aid England could offer. This "historic meeting of men mostly entirely ignorant of their subject," as Henry Wilson described it, finally agreed to send over an expeditionary force of four infantry divisions and one cavalry division, about 100,000 troops, under the command of Field Marshal Sir John French.[13]

Not until August 10, the day Emmich fought his way out of the inner city of Liége, did Colonel Huguet of GQG arrive in London with Joffre's request that the BEF be sent to the relatively forward area of concentration, Maubeuge–Le Cateau, an area much earlier determined by Huguet and Henry Wilson. Haig, for one, did not agree, and argued that the BEF should remain in England until "the campaign had actively opened," then go where "it would be most effective."[14]

Neither did Kitchener agree. Alone of the military hierarchy of England, France and Germany, this old soldier foresaw a long, difficult war. On August 7 he already had asked for "the First Hundred Thousand" volunteers to form a new army; now he argued that the old army should detrain at the less exposed destination of Amiens. Although he gave in to French and Wilson, who agreed with Joffre, he formally instructed Sir John: "It must be recognized from the outset that the numerical strength of the British Force and its contingent reinforcement is strictly limited, and with this consideration kept steadily in view, it will be obvious that the greatest care must be exercised towards a minimum of loss and wastage."[15]

When Sir John French sailed for France on August 14 he was at sixty-two a still fiery cavalry officer who had made a splendid reputation in the Boer War. Though time and the Curragh incident,[16] which forced him a few months earlier to resign as Chief of the Imperial General Staff, had somewhat banked his personal furnace, and despite the restrictive, rather confusing tone of Kitchener's orders, he reached France in a confident mood—he "hoped for the best and rather believed in it."[17] So did Colonel Huguet and so did the deputy chief of staff, Henry Wilson. Unfortunately the chief of staff, Sir Archibald Murray, was beset from the beginning with more doubts than a prospective bride on her wedding eve. Nor was the outlook of Douglas Haig, commanding I Corps, much better. Speaking of French and Murray in his diary Haig noted that "neither in my opinion is at all fitted for the appointment which he now holds at this moment of crisis in our country's history."[18]

But in Paris President Poincaré's optimism particularly impressed Sir John, and he retained the mood upon reaching GQG on August 16. After a briefing by General Berthelot the two commanders set about the work at hand. Joffre fully accepted French's independent command status—he could do little else—but explained his aggressive intentions for his left wing and asked French to co-operate as fully and quickly as possible. He then described Lanrezac as "the best commander in the French army," who would offer Sir John "complete support and skillful co-operation."[19]

French left Vitry-le-François, spent a night at Rheims and motored on to Lanrezac's headquarters at Rethel the next morning. He had been enormously impressed with Joffre, "a man of strong will and determination, very courteous and considerate," and no less impressed with the French General Staff officers, who struck him as "very deliberate, calm and confident." He now looked forward to meeting his new war neighbor, General Lanrezac.

Never an easy man, despite Joffre's description, Lanrezac by August 17 was suffering more ills than ever beset Job. The crux of his pain was the loss of what on the podium at the Staff College he had possessed in stifling degree: confidence. The lion of the French Army, he had gone to war without his teeth; now with the enemy building up before him all he could do was roar. He roared at Joffre's blindness and he roared about the delayed arrival of the BEF and what he sounded was his own fear of not being able to cope with the job he had been given. Lanrezac was scared.

Scarcely were French and his party out of their cars when Hely d'Oissel, Fifth Army chief of staff, turned to Colonel Huguet and apropos of the British Army remarked, "At last you're here; it's not a moment too soon. If we are beaten we will owe it all to you."[20] This cheery note struck the tone of the ensuing meeting. An Englishman hates to be surprised: his back put up by Lanrezac's unexpected brusqueness, French refused to commit himself to an earlier advance than the one scheduled, nor did he take kindly to the suggestion of subordinating Allenby's cavalry division to Sordet's corps.

Sir John's stubborn refusals coupled with his indistinct grasp of the situation increased Lanrezac's hostility. Shown the Intelligence map, marked with growing red lines called *chenilles* (caterpillars) to indicate enemy units, Sir John asked what the Germans were doing on the Meuse River. Lanrezac replied bitterly, "Why are they there? Why, to fish in the river." The sarcasm was not translated to the British field marshal, but Lanrezac's attitude showed plainly without it.[21]

Sir John left Rethel in an unsettled mood. Perhaps for the first time, with the red *chenilles* visible in his mind, he realized the enormity of Kitchener's instructions—or perhaps in the car taking him to Le Cateau he recalled his visit to German cavalry maneuvers in 1911, an impressive show brought home to him by the Kaiser's words: "It is not only the cavalry [that is the best in the world]; the artillery, the infantry, all the arms of the service are equally efficient. The sword of Germany is sharp; and if you oppose Germany you will find out how sharp it is."²²

Further unsettling news awaited French at Le Cateau, his new headquarters. That afternoon his old friend, General Sir James Grierson, commanding the II Corps, had died while en route to the front. But now an immense amount of work claimed the field marshal and some of his earlier ebullience returned upon seeing the splendid progress made in the concentration of his army. Despite Lanrezac and the red *chenilles* he had seen more good than bad in his hasty trip through France. Determined to keep his promise to Joffre he consulted with staff and commanders, then notified GQG that the BEF would advance on August 21.

Sir John's decision increased Joffre's hope for an early decision. On August 18 GQG Intelligence identified only two German cavalry divisions north of the Meuse and only four regular corps backed by three reserve corps to the south, with indications that at least a part of the southern formations was trying to cross the river between Liége and Huy.

To Joffre this information suggested two possible courses of enemy action: a march of the German right wing on both sides of the Meuse between Givet and Brussels, or a march with the bulk of the German strength south of the river against the left flank of Langle's Fourth Army.

Whatever the enemy movement, Joffre thought that his left was strong enough either to outflank or to hold the German right while his center, the Third and Fourth Armies, advanced against the main German concentration at Thionville–Metz.

To free the Third Army for this operation Joffre now created the Army of Lorraine, a force of predominantly reserve divisions taken from the Third Army and the Army of the Alps. Under the command of General Maunoury, a sixty-seven-year-old artillery officer who had commanded the War College and governed Paris before retirement, this force would protect the Third Army's right flank from any German attack out of Metz. Farther right the line seemed secured by Castelnau's and Dubail's offensive, while on the far right Pau reported Mülhausen in Alsace again in French hands.

Joffre received a slight setback to his plans when on August 19 he learned the Belgian Army was falling back from the Gette River onto Antwerp, thus severing contact with Sordet's cavalry and the fortress of Namur. But still not dreaming that a German build-up in any great strength was possible on his extreme left—GQG did not yet know Liége had fallen—he remained confident that the BEF and Lanrezac's Fifth Army could hold the left as he had planned.

His way cleared by the fall of Liége on August 16, Moltke now ordered the long-anticipated right-wing offensive: Hausen's Third Army to march west along the Meuse toward Namur, Bülow's Second Army and Kluck's First Army to cross the Meuse, march on the river Gette and cut the Belgian Army's retreat to Antwerp. For the latter mission Moltke subordinated Kluck to Bülow, an order displeasing Kluck as much as Bülow's subsequent order for him to execute a flank attack against the Belgian left at Dienst in corps strength. Though Kluck argued that this maneuver was a waste of time, Bülow overruled him. On August 18 von Linsingen's II Corps pushed out toward Dienst.[23]

Kluck had a point. Even as the German armies poured into Belgium on August 18, the Belgian Army was commencing a general retreat on Antwerp, the personal decision of King Albert who preferred sacrifice to suicide. His decision came none too soon. On the same day, Kluck's army began to reach him to change an orderly retreat into a series of hotly fought rear-guard actions.

Although Quast's IX Corps hit the Belgian 1st Division at Tirlemont and badly mauled it,[24] the Germans were too late. All the planning, all the work went in vain when on August 20 the Belgian Army reached its heavily fortified sanctuary, Antwerp. Here it immediately formed a thorn not in the least dulled by the occupation of Brussels and Kluck's continued advance westward the same day. While Arnim's corps staged a massive "victory parade" through Brussels, Kluck quietly and grudgingly detached a reserve corps to take up permanent shielding positions against the flanking threat of Antwerp—a task Schlieffen had given to the *Ersatz* divisions now with Rupprecht's Sixth Army on the left.

Meanwhile Hausen and Bülow tied in before the fortified city of Namur. But now the cavalry sniffed out French concentrations (Lanrezac's Fifth Army) west of Namur behind the Sambre River, a challenge met by Bülow's turning his right and center southward. That night, August 20, new orders from Moltke: place Namur under siege, attack in conjunction with Hausen the French on the Sambre. According to Moltke between seven and eight French corps stood in the way. As for the British Army, "It is the view here that no important debarkations [in France] have so far taken place."[25]

Bülow followed orders. Forming an army detachment to besiege Namur, he simultaneously co-ordinated an attack with Hausen who would strike west across the Meuse, while the Second Army struck south to the Sambre. Bülow now turned his army south, ordered Kluck to turn as well and tie into his right flank.

The order caught Kluck moving southwest toward Lille–Tournai. This was Schlieffen strategy. It was well understood by Kluck and his chief of staff Kuhl, and both argued hotly with Bülow for its pursuance. But Bülow was commanding now and Bülow refused to yield: "otherwise the First Army might get too far away and not be able to support the Second Army at the right moment."[26]

With that Kluck turned south and began heading for the British Army that the Germans thought to be still in England. Here was a real mistake. It was Moltke's and Bülow's fault, and it started a chain of events that three weeks later would end in German failure at the Marne.

# THE TRAGEDY OF PLAN XVII

5  THE FRENCH DREAM ended on August 20.

Against Rupprecht's prepared defenses in Lorraine, Dubail
called up his reserve, pushed two brigades through his left in a
night march to take the bridges of the Sarre at Gosselming and
Oberstinzel, open the way to the German rear for his cavalry.

Tired by the advance of the last days through tortuous
terrain and increasing resistance, untrained for night operations,
confused in the strange hilly country of woods and lakes, the
French *poilus* advanced slowly. It was daylight before forward
units reached the objective, but still the point brigade surprised
the enemy, took Gosselming by fast bayonet assault. Then the
Germans woke up, machine guns split the quiet air, artillery
blasted from behind the Sarre. Sacrificing Gosselming to fury
the French fell back, regrouped, the cavalry behind, waiting.

Meanwhile far to the left Castelnau's Second Army stood
grouped for dawn attack, only to watch an early sun disappear
behind the smoke of a German artillery bombardment that
tore lives from left to right. Hard on through the early mist
the Bavarians charged, big, well-trained soldiers, to smash the
French lines, tear through Castelnau's right flank and cut his
liaison with Dubail. With his right gone and his center going,

Castelnau was finished. At 1000 he ordered a general retreat toward Nancy. The Battle of Morhange was over—in a few hours the French had suffered some 10,000 casualties.[1]

By this time the Battle of Sarrebourg had begun and Dubail was in trouble. While his flank brigade regrouped for a new try at the Sarre bridges, German artillery opened along his front. Five of Rupprecht's corps struck the French left and hurled the infantry back onto the cavalry, a confused retreat on two divisions, which had not bothered to dig in.

The Battle of Sarrebourg cost reputations, but it made a few. Maud'huy, commanding the 16th Division centered on Sarrebourg, fought with the fury of Achilles, his vulnerable tendon that of inferior numbers. Forced slowly back, he finally yielded, ordered a retreat to the heights behind him. But as his torn battalions left their dead and wounded in the dusty streets the survivors heard their band playing the *Marche Lorraine* and in front of it saw their proud commander standing at attention, taking them in review.[2]

Dubail knew by now that Castelnau was in trouble but he could not guess how much trouble. He himself was bending both on his left and dangerously weak right. Far from broken, he was still fighting from main positions when GQG reported Castelnau's retreat toward the Grand Couronné defenses fronting Nancy. Recognizing the inevitable, Dubail ordered his army back to the Meurthe River.

Castelnau's Second Army stood in full retreat before Joffre learned of the German counterattack. He greeted the news with quiet surprise, patiently waited for details. Bad as these were, he offered but a mental nod: at last the old general thought he had the picture.

He thought he had the picture because all the day of August 20 reports from his left confirmed beyond doubt an immense German build-up north of the Meuse. All the rumors and unconfirmed reports and contradictory indications suddenly in a great burst confirmed beyond mortal doubt German presence in the strength of five corps, three divisions and two brigades of cavalry.

The discovery did not frighten Joffre, it interested him: the strength had to come from some place, he reasoned, and that meant from the German short right, Thionville–Luxembourg. And now this enemy had broken out in Lorraine, a counterattack big enough to push back two armies. That strength, too, had to come from some place: obviously from the German center, Thionville–Metz.

Against a weak German center Plan XVII looked better than ever. Late that night Joffre ordered his center armies to march. Langle's Fourth Army was to strike through the Ardennes toward Neufchâteau, his right flank guarded by the Third Army, under Ruffey, marching toward Arlon.

Here was a force larger yet than that which undertook the first offensive. Against an estimated six corps and three cavalry divisions, Joffre was sending eight corps and three cavalry divisions. Once again the French commander sat back, not quite so confident, but still very hopeful.

Anchored on Metz, Crown Prince Wilhelm's Fifth Army joined with Duke Albrecht's Fourth Army to form the right center of Moltke's vast sweeping arm. Advancing slowly in conjunction with the three armies on their right, by August 18 they gained the eastern edge of the Ardennes forest. There they stopped while Hausen and Bülow invested Namur and prepared to attack the French on the Sambre, a period used by German Cavalry to explore the tangled terrain of the Ardennes and chart march routes for the oncoming infantry which on August 20 invested the tiny French fort of Longwy.[3]

On August 21 Wilhelm's cavalry observed the first French movements toward the Ardennes, while German aviators confirmed large forces marching up from the west. Wilhelm now gained permission from Moltke for a limited advance which he turned into a general forward movement, while Albrecht on his right alerted his units so that by the night of August 21 not six corps, as GQG estimated, but ten corps, or a difference of about 180,000 soldiers, plus two divisions of cavalry and six Landwehr brigades faced the unsuspecting French commanders.[4]

The battle started early on August 22 when Ruffey's center blundered through a cold fog to hit a German corps, itself waiting to attack the French. Though surprised, the French fought furiously until fog lifted to expose their open artillery pieces to hidden German guns. With their artillery almost immediately knocked out they succumbed to panic. In only a few hours Brochen's entire corps, Ruffey's vital center, was in retreat to Tellancourt miles away.[5]

Meanwhile the battle spread. On the right Sarrail's corps struck three German corps, a combined strength that had to tell the story the German way. Similarly, on the left a single French corps soon struck two enemy corps. By 1100 Sarrail was just holding while Ruffey's Third Army, far from being on the offensive, was fighting for its life.

With Ruffey stopped, Langle's Fourth Army on the left had to suffer and it did. Langle's mission, the capture of Neuf-château, rested on Lefévre's Colonial Corps, a hard-bitten spearhead of sun-blackened veterans, the best in the French Army. Without realizing his right was unguarded—the corps assigned here had turned in a vain attempt to help Ruffey—Lefévre pushed a brigade forward on the left, a division on the right; though separated by nearly impenetrable woods these forces were to meet on the outskirts of Neufchâteau for a final concerted assault.

The brigade, under Goullet, made it that far only to meet a solid corps of Hessian and Rhinelander peasants who moved swiftly to the attack. Fighting like devils, Goullet's veterans more than held their own while supposing the 3rd Division momentarily would appear on their right.

But north of the Semoy River at Rossignol the 3rd Division struck another German corps, to begin a horrendous battle of bayonet charge and countercharge lasting throughout the day.

The leading French brigade, surrounded and beaten to a pulp and its retreat cut, finally surrendered—a loss of more than 11,000 killed, wounded or captured, the division commander and many of the officers killed, most of the division artillery captured. Remnants of two brigades escaped with difficulty and with terrible losses into the darkness.[6]

The rest of Langle's huge army fared little better. Lefévre's disaster was compounded by a surprise German attack against Poline's XVII Corps that sent it flying pell-mell to the rear in a complete rout. This breach in turn caused Langle's other corps on the left to withdraw from positions that in some cases had been taken only with severe losses.[7]

Far from the smooth advance anticipated, the French Third and Fourth Armies in one day had been forced into precarious defensive positions along their entire front. But meager communications coupled with the very difficult Ardennes terrain prevented either Ruffey or Langle from forming an exact picture of the disaster. Langle reported Poline's rout to GQG as a "disorderly retreat," Lefévre's massacre as a "disorganization" of the Colonial Corps.[8] Ruffey estimated in his report that he faced three enemy corps and GQG informed Langle that he was fighting only three corps—in fact each army was fighting against five corps.[9]

Ordered by Joffre to "resume your offensive as soon as possible," Langle during the following two days found himself everywhere being pushed back. With Poline's corps far to the rear, its units demoralized, and with Lefévre's corps down nearly to division strength, little choice presented itself. By the night of August 24 the two armies stood in retreat to the Marne.

While Ruffey and Langle were advancing in the Ardennes the vanguard of Lanrezac's Fifth Army reached the valley of the Sambre considerably far forward to the north.

In no better frame of mind than earlier, Lanrezac at headquarters some thirty miles to the rear could not decide what to do. Unwilling to cross the river, even to gain the northern commanding heights, until Langle came up on his right and the BEF on his left, he finally pushed two corps through the wretched industrial villages of the Borinage to establish outposts at the numerous bridges between Namur and Charleroi. He then placed a third corps together with Sordet's already exhausted cavalry on his left and assigned his final corps to the right where it faced east to guard the Meuse (which turns sharply to the south at Namur) until Langle's arrival. But his orders, particularly to his center corps, were vague, he neglected to bring up artillery to register on the vital bridgeheads and he left himself no reserve.[10]

Coming over the heights north of the river the next day, two German corps of Bülow's Second Army made up Lanrezac's mind for him. Though the German commanders had been ordered to stop at the Sambre River until Hausen's Third Army attacked the line of the Meuse from the east, they took one look at the weak French *picquets* and moved to the attack. By nightfall of August 21 German assault battalions had fought their way across the river at two points, slim spearheads that grew to major thrusts the next day.

Determined to throw the invader back across the Sambre, Defforges brought up the reserve of his X Corps and sent a regiment to assault the river village of Aubelais. With no preliminary artillery fire but with "bugles blowing, drums beating and flags flying," the *poilus* lowered bayonets and at the word "Charge" rushed headlong across open, flat ground. German Maxim machine guns chattered a welcome of bullets that tore through the young French bodies until what was left of a battalion reached the outskirts of the position, bayoneted one gun crew, then fell or somehow crawled back to where they had started.[11]

Savage fighting, stupid perhaps, but very brave, and on the left the same sort, where despite frantic efforts Sauret's corps yielded four or five miles during the day.

Lanrezac missed the play on the 21st, but the next day he woke up and faced a threat to his right by turning d'Esperey's corps north. This left the Meuse River line unguarded, so now he ordered up a reserve division to screen east toward the river until Langle's army reached him. But on August 23, instead of Langle's army, advance units of the German Third Army struck from the east, battered their way across the Meuse —a spearhead aimed at Lanrezac's weak right, and one that could only be countered by moving d'Esperey's corps right back where it came from.[12]

All that same day Lanrezac's left furiously fought the advancing enemy hordes. He himself was there. While a German Albatross single-seater circled overhead directing salvos from Bülow's 150-mm. howitzers, while attack and counter-attack claimed the field, the old professor, clad in red breeches and black tunic, pince-nez perched delicately on the broad nose, stood with hands folded behind his back, silent, staring at the German columns that never ceased coming, staring at the bodies covering the field, saying nothing, just silent and staring.[13]

And in the afternoon back at Army Headquarters Lanrezac learned that Namur had fallen, which meant more enemy divisions coming his way. And then he learned the British were heavily engaged on his left, and that meant still more enemy divisions. That night late the French Fifth Army commander, like his colleagues at Alsace and Lorraine and in the Ardennes, faced the inevitable and ordered a general withdrawal south.

Lanrezac's bridge outposts were under attack on August 21 when the BEF began its march toward Mons, an interim position where it would tie into Fifth Army's left before swinging on Soignies. With Allenby's cavalry screening to the northeast, the long columns marched the cobblestone roads in easy step to *Tipperary* until in late afternoon the points began to close the dismal mining area.

As Haig's vanguard deployed along a seven-mile front between Peissant and Mons, the II Corps, commanded now by General Sir Horace Smith-Dorrien,[14] began to string out behind the narrow, placidly green water of the Mons–Condé canal, an immense front of twenty-one miles running awkwardly through rubble and still-smoking slag heaps that offered little cover, a terrible stink and tremendous hindrances to unit movement.

Columns were still closing the new position early on August 22 when Sir John French left for a conference with Lanrezac at Philippeville, an effort frustrated by long columns of French infantry and artillery everywhere blocking the narrow roads. Obviously disorganized, their march tired and slovenly, they were heading south—they were retreating. Back at his own headquarters the old field marshal found cavalry reports of numerous contacts with the enemy to the northeast, a portent more than confirmed during the day by Henderson's aviators and Bülow's cannon sounding to the east. In the afternoon he learned the truth from Lieutenant Spears, his liaison officer to Fifth Army, who reported the Fifth Army's plight on the Sambre. One of Lanrezac's staff officers accompanying Spears then delivered his commander's request for the BEF to attack north of the Sambre and relieve the pressure on the Fifth Army. French could consider no such action, of course, and rightly refused; he did agree to maintain his present position at Mons for another twenty-four hours.

Despite the cannon to the east and the rumors circulating through the ranks to staff and back again, war seemed still quite far away the next morning, a Sunday. Men woke to rain and drizzle but this cleared to sun by the time ringing church bells filled the drab streets of the villages with stiffly dressed miners and their families, seemingly unconcerned with the khaki-clad intruders and the horse-drawn guns and the sweating, cursing gunners trying to hide their pieces with no place to hide them.

Early that day Sir John drove to Smith-Dorrien's headquarters, Haig and Allenby joined him, and the commander and his generals reviewed the situation. All agreed the present position was adequate in case of attack. Leaving Murray there with "full instructions as to arrangements which must be made if a retreat became necessary,"[15] the old cavalry officer drove off to Valenciennes to watch the arrival of the 19th Infantry Brigade, a new unit formed from rear-area units. Soon after he had left, Kluck's First Army attacked.

On the previous afternoon Kluck had suspected he was running into the BEF after his point brushed with the 4th Dragoon Guards and a British plane had been shot down in German territory. Supposing now that the British had landed at Calais, he had no idea of their strength and at once grew apprehensive of a flank attack. When early the next morning Marwitz reported enemy units detraining at Tournai, Kluck held up his advance until these were identified as a French brigade. Under way once more, he learned from patrols that afternoon that the British were defending in force at Mons. Without waiting for all of his corps to come up he decided to attack.

Quast's IX Corps hit the weakest part of Smith-Dorrien's weak line, the salient projecting north of Mons. After a heavy artillery bombardment the gray infantry bunched in from all sides, a mass attack shredded by cool rifle fire so accurately and rapidly delivered that the Germans believed themselves to be facing machine guns.

While Quast regrouped and returned to the attack, Lochow's and Arnim's corps came out of the woods against Smith-Dorrien's center and left, again in mass attacks that were beaten back by British rifle fire, a tactical surprise as great as the heavy siege artillery that broke the Liége forts.

All afternoon the fantastic British fire held steady, but with the enemy closing in on the Mons salient Hamilton's 3rd Division finally had to yield. With that Fergusson drew back the 5th Division, which had given far more than it had taken. Although the British line was now compressed to nearly half its original length and had fallen back some two miles from the canal, it was the enemy who signaled cease-fire at the approaching darkness.

And with good reason. Years later a German writer would

remember Fergusson's stand, when "the enemy opened a murderous fire . . . the rushes became shorter, and finally the whole advance came to a stop."[16] Captain Bloem, commanding an assault company that day, would remember his regiment's losses—25 officers, over 500 men—and would remember, too, a forlorn group of soldiers singing in the night, *Deutschland über Alles*, and his battalion commander telling him, "You are the only company commander left in the battalion . . . the battalion is a mere wreck, my proud, beautiful battalion."[17]

The British got hurt, of course. Haig fared the best; he always had been called "Lucky" Haig and that day the I Corps was out of the battle, took a mere 40 casualties. But the II Corps took over 1500, and if Smith-Dorrien gave the enemy more than that it was slight compensation, for he had no replacements and it was a serious loss.

And while his men were fighting, while Fergusson's people were crawling back from the salient, while Hamilton's infantry lay over their Lee-Enfields and squeezed off round after round that held four divisions, while artillery shells from both sides were turning the Sabbath of Mons into a Doré etching of hell, and while the citizens of Mons and Jemappes and a dozen other villages were loading possessions of a lifetime into little carts—while all hell was bursting loose on the firing line, Sir John French was dictating a message to Lanrezac on his right:

I am waiting for the dispositions arranged for to be carried out, especially the posting of French cavalry corps on my left.
I am prepared to fulfill the role allotted to me when the Fifth Army advances to the attack. In the meantime I hold an advanced defensive position extending from Condé on the left through Mons to Erquelines, where I connect with the two Reserve divisions south of the Sambre.
I am now much in advance of the line held by the Fifth Army, and feel my position to be as forward as circumstances will allow, particularly in view of the fact that I am not properly prepared

to take offensive action until tomorrow morning, as I have pre-
viously informed you.

I do not understand from your wire that the XVIII Corps has
as yet been engaged and they stand on my inner flank.[18]

Thus at 1510 on the afternoon of August 23 the
commander-in-chief of the BEF was unaware of the fight
to his front. Apparently not too upset when he did learn about
it, he ordered the II Corps to stand on its lines and "strengthen
your position by every possible means during the night."[19]
But then a message from GQG warned him to expect an
attack the next day by three enemy corps and two cavalry
divisions, and about midnight Lieutenant Spears informed him
that Fifth Army stood in full retreat.

Furious at what he regarded as Lanrezac's duplicity, Sir
John now hastily ordered a general retreat south. Early on
August 24 Haig lined up every gun he had, loosed salvo after
salvo at the enemy while Fergusson and Hamilton disengaged
their tired divisions and slipped away. The Battle of Mons was
over, the retreat had begun.

# THE RETREAT: I

**6** A LESSER MAN than Joffre, even a greater man, might have broken. For four days the grim reports of Sarrebourg, Morhange, Virton, Ethe, Rossignol, Neufchâteau, Charleroi and Mons rained into the schoolhouse at Vitry, turned the earlier confident air to a deepening gloom preluding the death of Plan XVII.

For by August 24 the famous plan was finished, useless as yesterday's newspaper, but with results a good deal more lasting. Under its terms the French and British armies had moved forward, met the enemy, fought and fallen back. The actions in Lorraine and the Ardennes, on the Sambre and at Mons comprised the Battle of the Frontiers and together spelled an immense Allied defeat.

Some said the French took 300,000 casualties in those first weeks.[1] Perhaps the figure was too high, yet the correct figure was also too high to be published and it was high enough to fill thousands of hospital trains puffing throughout France and carefully avoiding Paris because the trains were so many, morale so shaky in the capital.

Everyone admitted a fantastic officer loss, but only long after the war did the official figure emerge: out of a total

44,500 active and reserve officers, 4,773 fell in August alone.[2] In but a day the BEF suffered 1600 casualties, but it was obvious enough that this was a mere beginning—like the French armies everywhere along the line the British were fighting sharp rear-guard actions against a much more powerful enemy.

The materiel loss could not be calculated, but it also was enormous. Dead and dying horses, smashed guns, machine guns, rifles, ammunition and supply trains, tons of equipment littered the valleys and slopes of Lorraine, the forest of Ardennes, the coal pits of the Borinage. From Alsace north families fled from farms and houses of a lifetime, the enemy moved into the rich mines of the Briey coal fields, moved through the fields of ripening wheat and autumnal orchards, now all deserted before them.

Joffre faced a big moment of truth on August 24. In his garden at Vitry he walked up and down, massive hands clasped behind his back, an intent look in the heavy face and light blue eyes. The big general in baggy red breeches and crumpled black tunic, white hair awry, was probably the loneliest man in the world on that day in 1914, and he was probably afraid without admitting it to himself.

What had gone wrong? Well, Plan XVII presupposed a certain enemy strength, but the enemy from the opening shot of the war proved much stronger, until finally, too late, Intelligence learned that German reserve corps were fighting alongside the regular corps. Just yesterday Joffre had warned Sir John French to expect three corps and two cavalry divisions on his front; now his staff officers were saying that the BEF could expect to be attacked by five corps and three cavalry divisions.

The Germans had fooled him, no doubt about that, and to make matters worse Plan XVII had calculated on a combat readiness that the French Army just didn't have. The *offensive à outrance* seemed to have brought considerable trouble with this business of the moral versus the material, the mind versus the bullet, because bullets by 1914 were spewing forth from modern rifles and machine guns to kill the bodies that held the minds, and the minds didn't seem to be able to do much about it.

Joffre held a pretty good idea by now of what had happened. His army commanders told him some, his liaison officers a good deal more. Keen but inept junior officers jumped to the attack without preparatory artillery fire, without guarding their flanks, without building temporary emplacements behind them. No more were the generals—far too many of them—setting them right, or co-ordinating division and corps attacks, or leading in any sense of the word. At Sarrebourg one of Dubail's corps commanders had run and so had one of Ruffey's at Longwy, and on the same day a division commander had panicked, then committed suicide. At Charleroi one of Lanrezac's corps commanders disappeared during a big scrap and God knows what might have happened if good old Roquerol, the artillery commander, hadn't taken over when he did.

Still, could you condemn a doctrine when men failed to understand it? Those who ran it were doing all right. Foch held at Morhange, retreated only on order; d'Esperey up north seemed to be doing a good job; Pétain knew all about the offensive but when it came to holding the Meuse as ordered he used his head and put his brigade in trenches and strung wire like a sensible fellow.

All right, he would deal with the fools. Minister of War Messimy had just telegraphed him that the only punishment for weak officers was "immediate sentence to death . . . eliminate the old fossils without pity."[3] He would not shoot them, but he would retire them. As for the young, the ones left alive, he already had sent out orders to senior commanders to stop the stupid excesses of the assault—not that he thought it would help very much.

It was all very good admitting the errors, his own and those of his staff and his commanders, but what about the

situation they had caused? Here were Dubail and Castelnau
defending from Belfort past the Grand Couronné and now
reporting a heavy German drive to the Moselle, Ruffey and
Langle fighting a rear-guard action to the Meuse, Lanrezac's
big army or what was left of its 300,000 people retreating on
Givet–Maubeuge, French moving back to Valenciennes–
Maubeuge and between the BEF and the Channel some seventy
miles of open front with d'Amade's three Territorial divisions
against all of Marwitz' cavalry and Kluck's right wing.

A precarious position, no doubt about that. But not
hopeless.

Two days before, the Russians said they had advanced
twenty miles inside East Prussia, so maybe that would relieve
a little pressure on the western front. Too, only a few days
earlier Castelnau's Second Army had seemed to be whipped, its
shattered ranks trying to reorganize behind a slim reserve[4]
defending from temporary emplacements that Foch had built
on the chain of ridges, the Grand Couronné, jutting out of
Nancy.[5] On August 21 Castelnau had reported his situation
as "very grave" and, "in the eventuality of a new retreat, I
shall fall back under cover of the guns at Toul, in the direction
of the Hauts-de-Meuse [that is, behind the Moselle River to
the heights fronting the Meuse River, a retreat of some twenty
miles]."[6] Joffre hadn't liked that and had told his commander
to hold fast for at least twenty-four hours. It was a good
order, for while the messages were flowing from Nancy to
Vitry the French *poilu* was discovering that he wasn't so
badly hurt after all, that if thousands of him had been killed
and captured many more thousands remained alive and
whole, and like a man who takes a nasty fall, lies stunned,
slowly revives, finds no bones broken and gets up to go about
his business, the French soldier was coming to, finding his
unit, and officers who had been wondering if the mess could
ever be cleared suddenly saw cohesion, saw companies grow
to battalions until divisions appeared, and late at night on
August 21 Castelnau was reporting:

The situation of the Second Army has materially and morally improved; the Army this evening is holding the *Grand Couronné* and the Meurthe [River] from Nancy to Luneville; the enemy has advanced very little; during the evening he was still twelve miles from the Meurthe. Yesterday he experienced serious losses . . . there is no more talk of falling back behind the Moselle.[7]

That was three days ago and now Castelnau and Dubail were counterattacking, God knew with what results, but nonetheless counterattacking. Well, with a little time and re-organization perhaps his left and center could do the same. They had been defeated, but not destroyed; the rope of his campaign had broken, no doubt of it, and now it had to be re-tied and now he would have to do it.

Very well—he would retreat, trade territory for time, fire commanders he thought had failed, try to scrape up a new mass of maneuver and, finally, try again to attack. He summed it up nicely in concluding his report of August 24 to the Minister of War:

We are therefore compelled to resort to the defensive, using our fortresses and great topographical obstacles to enable us to yield as little ground as possible.
Our object must be to last out as long as possible, trying to wear the enemy out, and to resume the offensive when the time comes.[8]

Where was the force to come from? The situation in Alsace had steadied, some of Pau's army could be transferred. With Ruffey falling back to the Meuse, Maunoury and his Army of Lorraine could be used. Some discussion here: Berthelot, alone of the staff still optimistic, wanted to position the new force behind Lanrezac's Fifth Army, then counter-attack to the northwest to hit Kluck's flank and rear and cut that army away from the main German force. Joffre objected: if Lanrezac failed to hold, if the Germans turned his left flank, which was entirely possible, then the French would not lose a battle, they would lose the war.

Instead, Joffre saw a slow retreat of his entire left, the movement pivoting on Ruffey's army at Verdun. On the 24th he ordered two reserve divisions rushed to d'Amade; if d'Amade could hold, if he could count on the British, if the BEF and the Fifth and Fourth Armies would withdraw slowly south, exploiting favorable terrain to make temporary stands, interdicting the vulnerable German columns with artillery fire favored by the open country . . . then time would be gained to position a new force in the region of Amiens to strike at Kluck's flank: "My conception was a battle stretching from Amiens to Rheims with the new Army placed on the extreme left of our line, outside of the British and in a position to outflank the German right."[9]

Joffre listened to Berthelot's arguments and to the discussion of his staff officers—he generally did—and then followed by the silent Gamelin he walked and thought and finally decided that he, not Berthelot, was right, and on the night of August 25 General Instructions Number Two went to his armies. Simultaneously the incredibly complex transfer of units began: two divisions from Alsace, two divisions from Paris, the headquarters of the VII Corps, two divisions and Maunoury himself from Lorraine.

But now Joffre received an order from Paris, from Messimy: "If victory does not crown our efforts and if our armies are forced to retreat, an army composed of at least three active corps must be directed upon the entrenched camp of Paris. . . ."[10]

Joffre did not have three corps to spare, and certainly not for the Entrenched Camp. Taking advantage of the loophole, "If victory does not crown our efforts . . . ," Joffre cast the order from his mind, unheeded, and turned again to the problem of salvation.

One of the numerous ifs of any victory was the BEF's co-operation with Fifth Army. To settle matters Joffre arranged a meeting with French and Lanrezac at BEF headquarters, St. Quentin, for the next morning. Perhaps Joffre sensed what in fact was true: that Lanrezac's retreat coupled with the British action at Mons had turned Sir John into a Mohammed of defeat. If so, the British field marshal was about to be approached by the mountain of French hope.

Five days of victory momentarily erased Moltke's fears and filled OHL with an irrepressible optimism surpassed only by that of the jubilant army commanders. First had come Rupprecht's report from Lorraine: 12,000 prisoners, 50 guns, "a complete victory" with the enemy in "complete retreat . . . in complete dissolution."[11]

Similar glowing messages poured in from the Crown Prince and Duke Albrecht in the Ardennes, from Hausen, Bülow and Kluck in Belgium until they formed an immense tidal wave of victory that smashed over OHL headquarters in Coblenz. By August 25 optimism had persuaded Moltke and his staff officers that not only had their armies fought a great battle in the west but that it had resulted in the "decisive victory" on which German plans rested.[12]

Under Schlieffen-Moltke strategy this was the moment to transfer six corps to the east. Already on August 21 Von Prittwitz, commanding the Eighth Army in East Prussia, had admitted a defeat at Gumbinnen. No more content to yield German soil than Joffre had been willing to give up French soil, Moltke replaced the cautious Prittwitz with the old fire-eating von Hindenburg whom he called out of retirement. To Hindenburg he assigned Ludendorff as chief of staff, the latter's reward for brilliant action at Liége.[13]

But Moltke already had relinquished control on his left, and now he had to pay for it. When he neither agreed with nor dissented from Rupprecht's demand to drive through the Trouée de Charmes on the heels of the broken French armies, Rupprecht seized on his ambiguous attitude, ordered the advance of the Sixth and Seventh Armies. But these had been hurt in the Lorraine battles worse than Rupprecht supposed: rather than springing forward to strike the French remnants the armies did not cross the border until the 24th. On the 25th, to their amazement, they found themselves being counter-attacked, a disagreeable surprise that precluded among other things any transfer of their strength to the east.

Moltke's center proved in slightly better shape than his left, but here again the phantasy of command claims soon became apparent. These armies too were hurt, and progress through the Ardennes to the Meuse slowed and then, again unexpectedly, ran into increasingly heavy opposition from the beaten French. The one corps taken from the Fifth Army for transfer to Russia was soon replaced; the corps marked for transfer from Albrecht's army was never touched.

Desperately Moltke turned to his right. Although he didn't know it the same fantasy applied there. While Kluck, Bülow and Hausen loaded the wires with victory reports, the BEF and Lanrezac's Fifth Army stood in reasonably ordered retreat south—hurt, but not nearly broken. Before the battles on the Sambre and Meuse and at Mons the three right-wing German armies had shed a total of five plus corps for investing and screening purposes and they were tiring by the time of the battles which further hurt them.

Yet Moltke decided to take his eastern force from them and ordered the two corps—one each from Hausen's and Bülow's armies—at Namur to entrain for Prussia.

In less than a month the strong right wing was reduced from seventeen to less than twelve corps—the heaviest fighting lay ahead.

No one knows how the story began, but any number of British soldiers said they saw her. She came, an angel riding a big white horse, and she wore the dress of the Virgin and carried God's flaming sword, and the night after battle when the II Corps lay in its lines waiting to be attacked, the Angel of Mons rode down from Heaven and faced the German Army and refused to let it advance.[14]

Unfortunately for God's chosen children she left with

the dawn and Haig's cannon took over. It was not easy going for the II Corps. The order to retreat was delayed and at Andrecies a battalion of Cheshires who failed to get the word were surrounded, with only two officers and two hundred men escaping out of a thousand. Near Elouges a German attack hit the 15th Brigade in flank, another 1100 casualties. By nightfall of August 24 Smith-Dorrien was missing 3800 men, nearly 17 per cent of his combat strength.[15]

Considering everything, the troops took it well. While rear guards held Kluck to a three-mile advance, the long columns of young, very tired, very hungry reserve soldiers slogged south through refugee-choked roads seemingly endless under a hot August sun.

Sir John wasn't quite sure where they should go at first, but he was under no illusions as to his position. In a report that day to Kitchener he wrote, "I think that immediate attention should be directed to the defense of Havre."[16] For a time he toyed with marching his force on Maubeuge, gave that up and finally ordered the retreat south toward Le Cateau. But now the thick Forest of Mormal, ten miles long and six miles wide, loomed squarely in the line of retreat. On August 25 the BEF split, Haig's I Corps taking the roads across the Sambre on the right, Smith-Dorrien and the 19th Brigade falling straight back with Allenby's cavalry on the left. Meanwhile Snow's newly arrived 4th Division was coming up to Solesmes for further protection.

Lanrezac's retreating columns and the winding Sambre River delayed Haig's march, so that instead of in Le Cateau he bivouacked in Maroilles and Landrecies, villages eight miles east. About 1800 that evening, forward elements of Kluck's army struck Maroilles, a minor action soon broken off by the enemy; sometime later another German force attacked the Coldstream Guards at Landrecies, a brisk action that threw Haig's headquarters into panic: at 2200 he telephoned GHQ, "Attack heavy from northwest; can you send help?"[17]

GHQ reacted instantly: Archibald Murray fainted, Henry

Wilson took over and Sir John French telegraphed Smith-Dorrien to send help to Haig—if nothing else at least the 19th Brigade.

This was no time to bother Smith-Dorrien. Early that day Sordet's cavalry, passing from east to west, combined with thousands of refugees to delay his retreat until Kluck again fell on his rear guards. With sharp fighting at half a dozen points, by nightfall his command spread from Solesmes to Le Cateau, with only a portion of the units in position on the rolling fields south of the town. Far from being able to send the 19th Brigade to Haig, Smith-Dorrien did not even know where it was. He did know that his corps of 60 per cent reservists was so far fighting the war for England all by itself.

Dog-tired after three days of combat, their feet torn from the blistering hot and hard roads, their equipment scattered from Mons to Le Cateau, their khaki thoroughly wet from an evening downpour, the Tommies of the II Corps but slightly resembled the neatly turned-out troops who had advanced to Mons singing *Tipperary*. And now with Kluck's eager columns pushing in from the north Smith-Dorrien also knew that to continue the retreat as ordered earlier by GHQ would require every bit of ability he possessed and a lot of luck besides.

He was still trying to locate his units at 0200 when Allenby rode in to report the strength and proximity of the enemy: if the II Corps were to escape, Allenby advised, it would have to move out before daylight. Wearily, Smith-Dorrien asked Hamilton if he could manage, learned that the 3rd Division could not march before 0900; Fergusson's 5th Division, Smith-Dorrien knew, was still dribbling into Le Cateau. Allenby himself reported the cavalry as done in and incapable of much help for a retreat.

Smith-Dorrien now made one of the most controversial decisions of the Marne campaign. At 0315 he sent French a message that the II Corps, together with Allenby's cavalry,

Drummond's 19th Brigade and Snow's 4th Division, would stand and fight.

Sir John received the message about 0500, after the facts failed to warrant Haig's panic. Of two minds, he replied ambiguously:

If you can hold your ground the situation appears likely to improve . . . although you are given a free hand as to method, this telegram is not intended to convey the impression that I am not as anxious for you to carry out the retirement and you must make every endeavor to do so.[18]

Swayed by Henry Wilson who argued furiously against the stand, French ordered Wilson to telephone new orders an hour or two later. Smith-Dorrien told him it was impossible to break off the battle because it already had started. "Good luck to you," Wilson answered. "Yours is the first cheerful voice I've heard these three days."[19]

Smith-Dorrien needed luck. Although his stand caught Kluck by surprise, the German commander attacked with intensity inflamed by exasperation.[20] For two days he had been trying to push the beaten BEF into Maubeuge and now suddenly British 18-pdrs. and powerful 60-pdrs. were challenging his artillery from one end of the line to the other. Hurrying up to the center of action Kluck attacked with one corps on his left, one in the center, and with dismounted cavalry on his right. Coming up behind the cavalry were two infantry divisions and, on the right, another corps—in all, some 140,000 Germans against 55,000 British.

While the artillery duel roared during the morning, Kluck's left corps worked through Le Cateau and the little villages and through the rolling fields neatly marked by bramble hedgerows to Smith-Dorrien's right, now very vulnerable because of Haig's continued retreat south. There the British 5th Division, its right covered by the 19th Brigade, fought like all fury only to take terrible losses compounded about noon by a precipitate order to retreat. Some units failed to get the word, others were too involved to make it matter; by afternoon most of Fergusson's guns and a good many small units had been knocked out.

The situation was worse on the British left, where the 4th Division, lacking cavalry, communication units, field

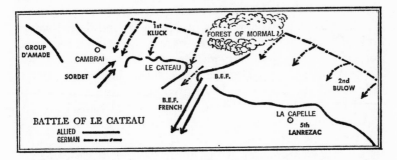

ambulances, engineers and, most important, field artillery, had come on the scene in a generally disorganized state. One of the officers there, B. L. Montgomery, later to become a field marshal but now a twenty-seven-year-old lieutenant in the 4th Division, remembered that,

On the early morning of the 26th August, 1914, the 10th Brigade to which my battalion belonged was bivouacked in the cornfields near the village of Haucourt after a long night march. One battalion was forward on a hill, covering the remainder of the brigade in the valley behind; we could see the soldiers having breakfast, their rifles being piled. That battalion was suddenly surprised by the Germans and fire opened on it at short range; it withdrew rapidly down the hill towards us, in great disorder.

Our battalion was deployed in two lines; my company and one other were forward, with the remaining two companies out of sight some hundred yards to the rear. The C.O. galloped up to us forward companies and shouted to us to attack the enemy on the forward hill at once. This was the only order; there was no reconnaissance, no plan, no covering fire. We rushed up the hill, came under heavy fire, my Company Commander was wounded and there were many casualties. Nobody knew what to do, so we returned to the original position from which we had begun to attack. If this was real war it struck me as most curious. . . .[21]

It was real war and it might very well have proved disastrous. Fortunately Sordet's cavalry, worn as it was, and the brave 84th French Territorial Division, weak as it was, met and briefly held the oncoming German reinforcement.

But by midafternoon, with his right and left folding, Smith-Dorrien ordered general retreat. Somehow exhausted commanders formed rear guards, slowly broke off action along the line. By evening the first columns began the sixteen-mile march to Reumont. Dead-tired and hungry, they now faced a heavy, cold rain. Behind them lay their chums, hundreds and thousands of dead, wounded and missing, tons of materiel, many of their guns. That day the 4th Division lost a quarter of its combat strength, the whole force suffered 8,000 casualties and lost 38 guns.

The survivors did not know, could not know how important this battle would prove to the BEF and thus to the war in France. They could not know that their sacrifice would mislead Kluck and would help to form his later and enormously vital decisions at the Marne. They only knew that they had fought and once more were retreating. They slogged silently into the night, wet, cold and hungry. There was no singing, only the shuffling sound of exhausted troops marching on command.

Had Kluck pursued he would have found easy pickings. But Kluck's soldiers had marched a long way, too; they were tired, some were hungry, many dead. As at Mons so at Le Cateau, the superb rifle and artillery fire of the British had torn jagged chunks through the gray-clad ranks. Still, they would have pursued on order, for they too were disciplined, but when no order arrived they were more than glad to sleep.

It was Kluck's fault. Believing he had met and beaten the entire BEF that day, he announced a great victory to OHL, told his troops they had taken 12,000 prisoners. Con-

vinced now that the BEF was based on Calais and that the
First Army thus sat astride its Lille–Cambrai communications,
he envisaged the beaten British divisions slinking westward
where his cavalry would check them until his army mopped
up their flank and rear.

Kluck was wrong. By morning the British were gone,
he had missed his chance. In one of the most amazing retreats
of the war, of any war, the II Corps and its ancillaries had
marched sixteen miles through hilly wooded country to
Reumont and, without rest, were continuing the retreat
twenty miles *south* through St. Quentin to Ham. When
Kluck's First Army moved out on August 27 it marched
*southwest.*

# THE RETREAT: II

7 MEN WERE DYING at Le Cateau when Joffre reached BEF Headquarters early on August 26. D'Amade, commanding the French Territorial divisions on the BEF's left, talked to him first, grave, unsettling words forming a fitting prelude to the conference.

Then the still pedantic if harassed Lanrezac appeared, pince-nez hooked over an ear "where they hung like a pair of cherries." Finding Joffre "wrapped in a cloak of enveloping dumbness" the swarthy Fifth Army commander rudely answered his senior's terse questions: yes, he had received General Instructions Number Two, but the close country of his march hindered effective artillery interdiction; besides how could you carry out anything with the unco-operative British on your left, their columns spilling over into your routes—very well, he would do what he could.[1]

Finally French and Murray joined the group. The calm, reasonably optimistic British field marshal whom Joffre remembered from Vitry was now plainly excited and pessimistic. Bitterly Sir John recalled how French estimates had placed the BEF in danger at Mons, how the Fifth Army's precipitate retreat left the BEF isolated, how right at this moment it was fighting for its life.

The diatribe bored Lanrezac, who accepted it with a shrug, no explanation, and soon left the meeting. Then a patient Joffre explained to Sir John that the French armies, too, had suffered, had faced and were facing calamity, but would survive. His new plan, he explained, depended very much on British co-operation; to insure that he would instruct Sordet's cavalry to attack to the utmost, would move up two more divisions of reserves to d'Amade's force. Lanrezac stood nearly ready to assume the offensive—all he, Joffre, asked of the BEF was to keep its place in the line.

Sir John did not understand about the new plan—what new plan? To Joffre's unexpressed annoyance, Murray, who had received it the previous night, had not yet given it to his commander.[2] Quietly Joffre went over its salient points, topped his words with a plea for French's co-operation. Sir John responded with a welter of doubts that drowned his half-hearted promise to hold. With a great many additional worries and with nothing whatsoever solved, Joffre returned to GQG.

Here he found new problems. Langle's Fourth Army, one of its corps nearly broken, was retreating behind the Meuse while on his right Ruffey's Third Army was fighting hard to hold position. That night more depressing news arrived from Huguet: "The British Army has met with defeat, and it now seems to have lost all cohesion. It will have to receive serious protection if it is to reorganize. . . ."[3]

Following this blow, Joffre learned early the next morning that Lanrezac planned a further retreat. Furious, he sent out a peremptory order to the Fifth Army commander to stand and fight at St. Quentin. Next he received General Maunoury, gave him command of the new force slowly assembling on the left, as yet only a few divisions euphemistically termed the Sixth Army, and ordered him to cover the British flank in conjunction with d'Amade's Territorials.

Notified of these moves the British commander replied that he was worried about English reaction to his losses. With the briskness of a medieval lord in the mead hall Joffre threw the British lion a propitiatory bone in the form of telegraphed gratitude for the British sacrifice,[4] a wasted effort because now Huguet reported a further retreat, indeed that French and Murray were thinking of a retreat to Compiègne where they wanted at least a week to reorganize the British Army.[5] Again Joffre drove to BEF, pled with French, returned disappointed to GQG only to learn that Millerand had replaced Messimy as Minister of War. Fortunately Millerand liked him—the war could proceed. Learning that new columns were approaching from the northwest and determined to take the pressure off the British, Joffre now ordered Lanrezac to change his planned attack from north to northwest, or across the British front. Admittedly a difficult task, Lanrezac accepted it with such violent objections that Joffre visited him at Marle the next morning.

Joffre found his Fifth Army commander a changed man: "Marks of fatigue lined his face; his color was sallow, his eyes bloodshot. . . ." In a matter of minutes he ripped Joffre's strategy to shreds, an attack so severe that Joffre, losing his temper, finally threatened to relieve him.[6] Leaving him with a written order to attack the next day Joffre again returned to his headquarters.

One crisis simply replaced another: Joffre now learned of new enemy columns advancing toward Rocroi, a considerable threat to Langle's left. Although Langle was putting up an increasingly good fight and wished to remain on the Meuse, Joffre ordered him to fall back, then transferred two corps, two reserve divisions and a cavalry division from him, formed them into an army detachment that shortly would become the Ninth Army, and gave them to Foch with orders to plug Langle's left.[7]

By the night of August 28 Joffre's entire stake lay with Lanrezac's counteroffensive at St. Quentin. It was going to come off, because Joffre's mind was made up to go to Marle to witness, if necessary to command, the vital offensive.

While Joffre prowled the field like a frustrated Napoleon, Moltke observed the swift action of his armies from far away in Coblenz. Kluck already had reported the victory of Le Cateau when the Chief of the Great General Staff issued a new General Directive on August 27 that continued the offensive along the entire front.

Despite severe resistance to his left wing and his transfer of two corps from the right, Moltke with this still showed a preference for his original strategy. Believing that the French left was retreating to the Aisne "with their extreme left pushed perhaps as far as St. Quentin, La Fère and Laon," Moltke ordered Kluck's First Army to "march west of the Oise toward the Lower Seine. It must be prepared to co-operate in the fighting of the Second Army. It will also be responsible for the protection of the right flank of the forces. . . ."[8] On the same day Moltke removed Kluck's army from Bülow's control.

Kluck meanwhile had lost the BEF, which retreated south while he advanced southwest. Although encountering slight resistance from d'Amade's Territorials and the first elements of Maunoury's Sixth Army, Kluck paid little heed to these forces and by 28 August was convinced that

the left wing of the main French forces is retreating in a southerly and southwesterly direction in front of the victorious Second and Third Armies. It appears to be of decisive importance to find the flank of this force, whether retreating or in position, force it away from Paris and outflank it. Compared with this new objective, the attempt to force the British away from the coast is of minor importance.[9]

In other words, strike the left flank of the French Army, roll it up and win the battle by destroying the enemy, a course of action Kluck now proposed to Bülow on his left: the First Army *would turn its advance from southwest to south* with the Second Army conforming.[10] Here is the genesis of what was to prove a decisive change in German right-wing strategy. As it turned out, soon after sending this proposal to Bülow, Kluck received Moltke's new Directive which removed the decision from his, Kluck's, hands. For the time being Kluck would conform, but from now on the new strategy was never far out of his mind.

Kluck's message found Bülow north of the Oise River with advance elements of his corps already across the river to his front and on his right moving easily through St. Quentin, down the left bank of the Oise.[11] Ignoring Kluck's proposal in favor of Moltke's new Directive, Bülow ordered a general advance for August 29 with La Fère, an obsolete fortress, as the day's objective. Although he didn't know it, Lanrezac's Fifth Army stood squarely in his path.

To fight the battle he didn't want, the scholarly old Lanrezac covered his right with cavalry, screened north with one corps, ordered another to attack northwest, while his left corps, its flank guarded by reserve divisions, attacked west toward St. Quentin.

It was not the best position and Lanrezac realized this. His left flank stood at least a day's march north of the BEF, and when Haig on the previous day volunteered to attack north to St. Quentin with his practically untouched corps, Lanrezac seized on the opportunity. Unfortunately that night Sir John French refused permission,[12] a decision that further infuriated Lanrezac, whose left, of course, remained in its precarious state.

The battle kicked off to the surprise of both sides. In early morning mist Lanrezac's point blundered into the enemy. Though surprised at contact, Bülow wasted no time in opening heavy artillery fire along his front and in committing his other two corps. By midmorning Lanrezac's center corps was calling for help while his two left corps were fighting hard without advancing.

Meanwhile Lanrezac and Joffre were acting out a strange

play at Laon, Fifth Army headquarters, eighteen miles south. Joffre arrived there at 0900, found Lanrezac's attitude much improved and wisely refrained from interfering with the battle. While Lanrezac, pince-nez hanging from an ear, dictated his orders Joffre strolled silently about headquarters, following reports filtering in from the field, now and again staring at the large map with the red *chenilles* crawling across the contours

of France. For nearly three hours the inscrutable general hovered about Lanrezac's headquarters like a bad conscience; then, satisfied that Lanrezac was doing his best, he repaired to the local railway station for noon dinner.

Unfortunately for the Allied cause, Lanrezac's best was insufficient, through no fault of his own. Eighteen miles away, with communications dependent on couriers, he failed to sense either of his center corps commanders' needs until early afternoon when he finally committed d'Esperey's corps.

It was none too soon. Though attack and counterattack ruled the field, the highly trained German troops were slowly gaining the edge of victory. A German survivor later recalled an example of the discipline demanded and gained in Bülow's army:

. . . A platoon of an adjacent company was ordered to advance towards a single tree on a hill. It started moving when suddenly enemy shells burst at some distance. The men, becoming bewildered, dispersed and sought cover behind a hay stack. This was observed by the division commander who stood directly in front of us. He hailed the platoon leader: "Lieutenant, that is the wrong way for your platoon to behave. Fall your men in, facing the bursts, and order them to manual of arms." The lieutenant called his men to, dressed them and ordered them to present arms. Then he commanded: "Rifles to the shoulder. Move out right and left. Direction: the single tree on the hill." The platoon then advanced in perfect extended order. . . .[13]

The French, too, played some tricks. Deciding to intervene between the two corps and lead them into combined counterattack, d'Esperey drew up his corps artillery, drenched the objective in shrapnel, then marched the regiments of his 1st Division around Le Herie and down the gentle, rolling, copse-studded slopes, their colors flying, the band playing the *Marseillaise*.[14] As this dashing commander supposed, the tired soldiers on the line surged forward in a general advance, highly successful but ended prematurely by darkness.

But on Lanrezac's left Valabrégue and Defforges had withdrawn across the Oise to abandon the principal attack. Positioned on Hache's line of retreat, de Mas Latrie's XVIII Corps had to be withdrawn, and with the left gone the front had to fall back. That night Lanrezac requested permission for a general withdrawal.

Joffre would have refused it a few hours earlier, but on his way back to GQG that night after another fruitless talk with French he met Henry Wilson. Wilson and Huguet had come from GQG where they had found Belin a nervous wreck, quite "out of it." Berthelot, fit and hearty as ever, listened carefully to Wilson's arguments against a prolonged stand at St. Quentin, then arranged the meeting with Joffre. Now in front of the cathedral at Rheims "the ugliest man in the British Army," as Wilson described himself, pulled no punches in his graphic analysis of the situation, particularly the overwhelming strength of the German right wing. Joffre was not inclined to listen—it was the only time in the campaign either Wilson or Huguet found him "tired and depressed"—but he held enormous respect for Wilson, who was a friend of France, and he did listen. And back at GQG at 2300 he approved Lanrezac's request to withdraw behind the Serre River.[15]

Had any doubt remained in Joffre's mind, events of the next day dispelled them. D'Amade was pushed back across the Somme, Maunoury's Sixth Army, still detraining, was forced to retire behind the Avre, French was preparing to retire miles south to Compiégne–Soissons, where he wanted at least ten days to reorganize, Lanrezac was retiring, Langle was struggling to hold the line of the Aisne and Ruffey, a nervous wreck, had to be relieved and replaced by Sarrail. Though Castelnau and Dubail were holding, indeed were fighting Rupprecht to a standstill, General Instructions Number Two, the plan implemented only five days earlier, was as dead as the old Plan XVII.

The situation plainly called for another knot and a hasty one. Joffre first appealed to Poincaré to bring diplomatic pressure on Sir John—a drastic measure in drastic times. He then decided to bring back his left profiled in a northwest direction to strike where and when he could between Kluck and Bülow. The respite caused by Lanrezac's stand at St. Quentin coupled with further retirement south would allow him to bring still more strength from the east to build up the Sixth Army. This was risky but he had to do it, and he also had to take a corps from the Fifth Army. Meanwhile he would base the Sixth Army on Paris to provide a mobile garrison for its defense. Since August 26 Galliéni, the newly appointed Governor of Paris, had been frantically trying to repair the neglected defenses of years and trying to figure some sort of defense with the scratch forces at his disposal.

By abandoning General Instructions Number Two Joffre admitted the poverty of his military fortune and by warning the government to leave Paris he added a blunt exclamation point. Yet even as he turned to the new maneuver events were shaping in his favor. The enemy also was coming to certain conclusions; and, across the Channel in England, so was the British Government.

The natural distrust of nations coupled with Lord Kitchener's innate sense of strategy accounted for the independent position of the BEF and the anomalous orders furnished its commander. The best military commander in the world endowed with the most skillful political gifts would have found the position difficult. To the British field marshal, a very proper, unimaginative cavalry officer who liked his situations black and white, it was impossible.

Charged with protecting the small, highly trained army, French saw its very existence threatened at Mons when Lanrezac's precipitate and unannounced retreat so dangerously left the British right exposed. Still seething by the time of his conference with Joffre and Lanrezac on August 26, French became infuriated at Lanrezac's rude behavior, then horrified when he learned something of his losses at Le Cateau. By August 27 he made up his mind: he was not going to see the BEF slowly fed to the enemy. On that day he alerted General Robb, commanding rear-area communications, to "his intention to make a definite and prolonged retreat, due south passing by Paris to the east or west."[16]

Sir John expressed almost none of his concern in his frequent telegrams and letters to Lord Kitchener, who thought the war was going quite smoothly. To ease the pressure in the west Churchill on August 27–28 landed a brigade of Royal Marines at Ostend, and they were still there on August 30 when Kitchener finished reading a fairly reassuring report from French, only to learn in a report from General Robb of French's intention of definite and prolonged retreat. Kitchener immediately queried French, who replied the following day:

I have decided to begin my retirement tomorrow in the morning behind the Seine in a south-westerly direction west of Paris. . . . I cannot say that I am happy in the outlook as to the further progress of the campaign in France . . . my confidence in the ability of the leaders of the French Army to carry this campaign to a successful conclusion is fast waning, and this is my real reason for the decision I have taken to move the British Force so far back. . . .[17]

At last the truth was out. To the old soldier French's attitude was "calamitous"; such a retirement, as Kitchener explained to a hastily summoned Cabinet, "might mean nothing less than the loss of the war." The Prime Minister and Cabinet agreed; on August 31 Kitchener wired his field commander that the Government "expect that you will as far as possible conform to the plans of General Joffre for the conduct of the campaign. . . ."[18]

French's telegraphed reply aptly summed up his attitude:

If the French go on with their present tactics, which are practically to fall back right and left of me, usually without notice, and to abandon all idea of offensive operations, of course then the gap in the French line will remain and the consequences must be borne by them. I can only state that it will be difficult for the force under my command to withstand successfully in its present condition a strong attack by even one German army corps. . . . An effective offensive movement now appears to be open to the French, which will probably close the gap by uniting their main flanks. But as they will not take such an opportunity I do not see why I should be called upon again to run the risk of absolute disaster in order a second time to save them. . . . I think you had better trust me to watch the situation and act according to circumstances.[19]

Kitchener ignored the advice, left for France that night. On September 1 the two field marshals met at the British Embassy in Paris. For a time, a rather short time, French vented his anger on his venerable senior. When the conversation boiled Kitchener took him to another room away from Murray, Huguet, Ambassador Bertie, Viviani and Millerand. Little doubt exists as to who did the telling in this *tête-à-tête*. Kitchener's piercing blue eyes might have faded since Egypt days, but he was never far removed from the conqueror of

Omdurman who once thought to use the Mahdi's skull for a drinking cup;[20] French might have been his favorite officer but now the honor of England was at stake. England's trust of Kitchener almost "savored of religious allegiance," and earlier when he informed Churchill of Sir John's implied intention to retreat, "it was," said Churchill, "like seeing old John Bull on the rack."[21]

That night Kitchener sent French a letter:

After thinking over our conversation today I think I am giving the sense of it in the following telegram to the Government: "French's troops are now engaged in the fighting line, where he will remain conforming to the movements of the French army, though at the same time acting with caution to avoid being in any way unsupported on his flanks."

I feel sure you will agree that the above represents the conclusions we came to; but in any case, until I can communicate with you further in answer to anything you may wish to tell me, please consider it an instruction. . . .[22]

Although Bülow admitted 6,000 casualties at Guise–St. Quentin, he was not to be outdone by the victorious claims of his royal neighbors. On August 30 he informed OHL of a "complete victory" and simultaneously signaled Kluck on his right: "Enemy decisively beaten today; strong forces retiring on La Fère. The British, who were barring the Oise, are also retreating, some in a southerly, some in a southeasterly direction." That evening he told Kluck, "To gain the full advantage of victory, a wheel inward of the First Army pivoted on Chauny toward the line La Fère–Laon is urgently desired."[23]

Kluck received this when his First Army was marching to the Avre River, a southwesterly course prescribed by Moltke's August 27 Directive and one not unduly hindered by the ragtail forces before him. Bülow's message jibed with Kluck's earlier suggestion except that the sharp turn east now proposed by Bülow did not seem logical if the flank and rear of the retreating French were to be attacked. Instead, Kluck decided to turn southeast, his right flank protected by Gronau's IV Reserve Corps. He then learned that Bülow would rest on August 31—a strange development after a "complete victory," but one seeming not to affect his own plans, which he radioed OHL.

At OHL, moved now to Luxembourg, only about 150 miles away from the First Army, Kluck's message found Moltke in two minds. Continuing operations along the battle line had rubbed the gloss off the "complete victories" earlier reported; in fact, Rupprecht had given ground in Lorraine. Then the sorties of the Belgian Army from Antwerp tossed in a sobering thought, until on August 29 Moltke was complaining in a letter to his wife of the Emperor's "hip-hip-hooray attitude." On August 30 he learned of the British landing at Ostend, the vanguard, it was rumored, of an expeditionary force of 80,000 Russians or two corps to fall on his thinly shielded lines of communication.

Against these "alarums and excursions" stood Albrecht's message of August 30—the passages of the Meuse were forced, a "great victory," the French armies routed. Next came Bülow's message announcing "complete victory" at St. Quentin, an intercept of Bülow's message to Kluck suggesting he turn east, and finally Hindenburg's confirmation of the Tannenberg victory in Prussia including the complete destruction of an entire Russian army.

In Moltke's mind his task more than ever was to eliminate the French Army. Obviously he lacked troops either for a drive west of Paris or to invest Paris, but this no longer seemed necessary.

With Kluck encountering only slight resistance, with the British obviously defeated, the main French strength lay in front of his center armies. If Rupprecht could break through on the left and Bülow and Kluck on the right, Moltke would win a classic envelopment battle.

Accordingly he now approved the change of direction of his right wing: Bülow to march toward Rheims, Kluck toward Compiégne–Noyen.

Here was a decision of supreme importance, for with it Moltke forever traded Schlieffen for mere tradition.

# " . . . THE HONOR OF ENGLAND IS AT STAKE"

**8** Kluck was still north of Paris when British air and French cavalry late on August 31 reported his change of direction to the southeast. Maunoury, commanding the Sixth Army, at once asked Joffre for permission to attack Kluck's flank.

Though interested, Joffre declined to act prematurely: the Sixth Army was still too weak, the British stood two days' march south of the Fifth Army, he had no reason to believe he could count on Sir John French, and at the moment a cavalry incursion from Soissons was threatening Lanrezac's left.[1]

On September 1 Joffre still regarded Maunoury's mission as the defense of Paris while his other armies fell back to rest and reorganize, a plan formalized in General Instructions Number Four, issued that day from GQG, now moved to Bar-sur-Aube. Prescribing the limits of retreat as the Aube and the Seine, but without implying they need be reached, the new Instructions left no doubt of Joffre's ultimate intentions: "As soon as the Fifth Army escapes the threat of envelopment against its left, the whole of our Third, Fourth and Fifth Armies will resume the offensive."[2] Joffre also asked Minister of War Millerand for and received control of the Entrenched Camp of Paris, "to enable me, if the case arises, to employ the mobile part of the garrison [the Sixth Army] in field operations." He concluded the Instructions with ". . . finally the mobile troops of the Entrenched Camp of Paris may also take part in the general action." To answer the threat to Lanrezac he scraped up a cavalry corps, gave it to Conneau with orders to shield the Fifth Army's threatened left.

Soon after issuing the new Instructions Joffre ran smack into an old problem, Sir John French. During his conference with Kitchener in Paris the British field marshal gave Minister of War Millerand his own strategic plan in the form of a letter now forwarded by Millerand to Joffre. In broad if not vague terms French proposed a line of defense "which would run along the river Marne and stretch a few miles to the west and north-west of Paris." If Joffre accepted this, French would hold the BEF in the vicinity of Nanteuil, but "not a moment should be lost in beginning the construction of defenses for the position, using all the resources at our command."[3]

Joffre refused the proposal for several reasons. Although air reports on the evening of September 1 and a secret map captured from a German officer suggested that Kluck was across the Oise River marching southeast or *away* from Paris, reports on September 2 had him again moving on Paris. In any event Joffre did not want a static defense. Finally, by the time the British field marshal returned to GHQ late on September 1 the war had caught up with him.

At Néry early in the day a German cavalry division including twelve guns jumped a British cavalry brigade supported by a single battery of Royal Horse Artillery, a short but very sharp action costing 150 British lives but giving the defenders 8 of the 12 enemy guns. Similar sharp actions at Crépy-en-Valois and Villers-Cottérêts caused Sir John to retreat further to Dammartin, an action that was being carried out while Joffre was studying the British commander's plan.[4]

Still, Sir John's implied change of attitude was welcome.

With the utmost tact Joffre explained why he could not change his present plan, which asked the BEF to help defend Paris by crossing the Marne, blowing the bridges and forming a front along the Seine River until the Fifth Army attacked.

The question of the long-awaited counteroffensive remained very much alive at GQG. Colonel Dupont and the Operations Section wanted to organize it without delay; Berthelot wanted to retire behind the Seine because of troop fatigue; Belin wanted to hold off until the fog of war cleared.

Joffre agreed with Belin, but as a preliminary move decided to get rid of one of his biggest headaches. On September 3 he went to Lanrezac's headquarters and in two sentences relieved him of the Fifth Army command, which he gave to Franchet d'Esperey. Back at GQG he telegraphed his decision to Huguet:

Inform Marshal French that General Franchet d'Esperey has been placed in command of the Fifth Army. He has orders to act in close and cordial relations with the Field Marshal. I have great hopes on this understanding.

To Galliéni he later wrote,

I have sent General Lanrezac . . . to report to you. . . . You must not pay any attention to his pessimism, which makes him see only the risks involved in an operation and paralyzes his initiative. . . . I put him at your disposition; do what you like with him.[5]

When Joffre wrote this letter, about 0300 on September 4, the German right-wing movement had revealed itself enough for him to take another propitiatory step vis-à-vis the BEF. In the same letter to Galliéni he wrote,

A part of General Maunoury's active troops can be pushed to the northeast at any moment from now on, so as to threaten the right flank of the Germans and thus give the British left the feeling that they are being supported on this side. It would be useful to inform Sir John French of this and also to keep in constant touch with him. . . .

Despite the almost certain fact of Kluck's march to the Marne, Joffre was still being cautious. He had to be. Late on September 3 Foch in speaking of the Ninth Army's combat readiness "considered it premature to undertake any offensive action for several days." Langle, nearly as aggressive as Foch, had just requested rail transport for the further retreat of the XII Corps, such was its condition.

But beginning on September 4 events hurled themselves against the hours. A letter from French confirmed his full understanding of Joffre's plan and the part the British Army was to play in it. About midmorning General Clergerie, Galliéni's chief of staff, telephoned from Paris. Kluck definitely was continuing his advance southeast, was accentuating it; Galliéni wanted to move Maunoury's Sixth Army east, with the BEF marching on its right toward Monterau.

The message found GQG hotly arguing the situation. Berthelot still wished to hold off, then launch a general attack by the Fifth and Ninth Armies to the northwest and by the BEF and the Sixth Army to the north (his old idea). Refusing him, Joffre approved Galliéni's request and, in reply to another message from Paris, directed the Sixth Army to move "to the left bank of the Marne south of Lagny."

Impressed with Berthelot's fear that the Fifth Army was incapable of performing a virtual about-face, Joffre telegraphed its new commander, d'Esperey:

Circumstances are such that it may be to our advantage to deliver battle tomorrow or the day after against the German First and Second Armies with all the forces of the Fifth Army in conjunction with the British Army and the mobile elements of the Paris garrison. Please inform me whether you consider your army to be in condition to undertake this attack with chances of success.

To Foch on d'Esperey's right he sent a liaison officer with instructions to brief the Ninth Army commander and report his reaction.

But now French, urged by the cautious Murray, under-

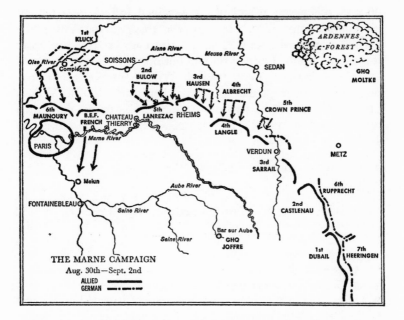

THE MARNE CAMPAIGN
Aug. 30th—Sept. 2nd

went a change of heart. Huguet reported the BEF would hold its present positions during the day but on September 5 would continue its retreat some miles behind the Seine. This development, coupled with increasing reports of strong German columns crossing the Marne at Château-Thierry to threaten d'Esperey's left wing, decided Joffre to delay any offensive for another five or six days.

But subordinate meetings between various commanders were radically changing matters. After receiving Joffre's approval to move out the Sixth Army, Galliéni hurried to Melun to co-ordinate the action with French. There he found only Murray, who greeted him unenthusiastically. Though promising to give Sir John a jointly prepared memorandum calling for BEF co-operation, Murray that evening—French still being absent—ordered the BEF to continue its retreat.

While this meeting was taking place Henry Wilson caught

up with d'Esperey, who had just received Joffre's query about his combat capability. Handing the message to Wilson the French commander said, "I am going to answer that my army is ready to attack. I hope you will not oblige us to do it alone."[6]

Enthusiastic as ever, the tall Wilson jumped at the opportunity and together they worked out details. Wilson promised to do his best to persuade Sir John to the plan, then he left for Melun and d'Esperey reported the arrangement to Joffre:

1. The battle cannot begin before the day after tomorrow, September 6.

2. Tomorrow, September 5, the Fifth Army will continue its withdrawal on the line Provins–Sézanne. The British Army will execute a change of direction facing east, on the line Changis–Coulommiers and to the southwards, provided its left flank is supported by the Sixth Army, which should reach the line of the Ourcq north of Lizy-sur-Ourcq tomorrow, September 5.

3. On September 6 the general direction of the British offensive would be Montmirail, that of the Sixth Army Château-Thierry, that of the Fifth Army Montmirail.

In a separate message he wrote:

In order for the operation to succeed, it is necessary:

1. To be able to count upon the close and complete co-operation of the Sixth Army, which must debouch on the left bank of the Ourcq, northeast of Meaux, on the morning of the 6th.

2. For the Sixth Army to reach the Ourcq tomorrow, September 5; otherwise the British will not march.

My army can fight on the 6th, but its condition is far from brilliant. There is nothing to be expected from the three reserve divisions.

It would be well if Foch's Detachment [the Ninth Army] could vigorously participate in the action; direction, Montmort.[7]

For one having been in command of the Fifth Army only twenty-four hours, d'Esperey showed a keen appreciation of the situation and tremendous personal resolution. His messages omitted one fact, however. Wilson's promise to try to influence Sir John had been taken by the optimistic d'Esperey as a definite commitment. Joffre nonetheless was impressed—he later wrote it was d'Esperey who "made the Battle of the Marne possible"—and now, having also received Foch's affirmative reply, he directed Gamelin to prepare General Instructions Number Six, but fixed the date for the counter offensive as September 7. When that evening Galliéni telephoned objecting to the order for Maunoury to advance south of the Marne—Galliéni already had ordered him to advance north of the river—Joffre informed him of the new plan and agreed that Maunoury should proceed with Galliéni's order. Since Maunoury's advance would probably alert the enemy, Joffre then changed the date of attack to September 6.[8]

No sooner was the new order issued than d'Esperey's and Wilson's false optimism brought crisis: about 2300 Huguet telegraphed from Melun—Sir John French, alarmed at the continuing changes, preferred to study the entire question before committing himself. His army was continuing its retreat.[9]

Weary beyond description, Joffre sent Major de Galbert, a personal aide, to Melun with a copy of the new Instructions. The next morning, without waiting for de Galbert's return, he oriented Millerand and asked him to have French approached through diplomatic channels. Then de Galbert returned, his mission a failure—he had not been allowed to see French. Joffre now left for Melun.

Flanked by three of his staff officers, including Gamelin, the old general met the old field marshal in the Château Vaux-le-Pénil. In a salon stripped for wartime purposes Joffre quietly and slowly stated his case. His voice rose slightly at the peroration:

"So far as regards the French Army, my orders are given and whatever may happen I intend to throw my last company into the balance to win a victory and save France. It is in her name that I come to you to ask for British assistance, and I urge it with all the power I have in me. I cannot believe that the British

Army will refuse to do its share in this supreme crisis—history would severely judge your absence."

Joffre stared at Sir John for a long moment, suddenly banged his fist on the table. *"Monsieur le Maréchal*, the honor of England is at stake!"

Visibly shaken, French hesitated a moment, then said, "I will do all I possibly can." With that he served tea.[10]

Convinced that his arguments had won the field marshal over, Joffre returned to his new headquarters at Châtillon-sur-Seine, where in his office, a monk's cell in a convent, he signed an order long awaited by his troops and himself:

We are about to engage in a battle on which the fate of our country depends and it is important to remind all ranks that the moment has passed for looking to the rear; all our efforts must be directed to attacking and driving back the enemy. Troops that can advance no further must, at any price, hold on to the ground they have conquered and die on the spot rather than give way. Under the circumstances which face us, no act of weakness can be tolerated.

J. JOFFRE[11]

With Bülow's Second Army resting on its dubious gains and with meagre reports coming in from Kluck's First Army, Moltke in Luxembourg turned his attention increasingly to his center armies. Completely misled by the steady flow of victory reports, both he and nearly everyone at OHL were becoming convinced that the great decision could soon be reached by the Fifth, Fourth and Third Armies. But Moltke could not ignore Intelligence reports of troop movements behind the French armies and of enormous activity in the Entrenched Camp of Paris. Rightfully worried, but without telling Bülow and Kluck why, he notified them on September 2,

The French are to be forced away from Paris in a southeasterly direction.
The First Army will follow in echelon behind the Second

Army, and will be responsible henceforward for the flank protection of the force.

The appearance of some of our cavalry before Paris, as well as the destruction of all railways leading to Paris, is desirable.[12]

This order found Bülow licking his wounds between the Aisne and the Marne, his army stretching from Vesle on the left to Soissons on the right. Kluck's advance guards were probing Château-Thierry, a day's march ahead of Bülow, and his remaining corps were approaching rapidly. Kluck could have used the rest, for on that day his continual twenty- to twenty-five-mile daily marches were telling, as noted by one of his officers:

The men stagger forward, their faces coated with dust, their uniforms in rags, looking like living scarecrows. They march with their eyes closed, singing in chorus so that they shall not fall asleep. . . .[13]

But to Kluck the new order meant a halt of at least a day while Bülow's army came up on his left, when his whole mission, *in his mind*, was to strike the French Fifth Army's flank while Bülow pushed in its front. This, taken with victories of the other armies, would yield total victory. To halt now would mean only the Fifth Army's escape or, as he put it to OHL, "the proposed driving of the enemy from Paris in a southeasterly direction could only be carried out by the advance of the First Army."

Certain of his own strategy and convinced of OHL's confusion, Kluck simply refused the order to stop his advance, wait for Bülow to come up, then "follow in echelon behind the Second Army." He did position one reserve corps and an understrength cavalry division to his right rear as flank guard. But when his leading corps pressed across the Marne the next morning the First Army commander ordered the other corps to follow, with one in echelon on his right as a further shield, toward Paris.

This was insubordination of the utmost importance, for

now Kluck's right flank—the right flank of the entire German line—stood exposed to attack by Maunoury's Sixth Army.

Kluck was closing the Petit Morin River and Bülow had crossed the Marne when on September 4 Kluck's message reached Moltke. At last the German commander-in-chief was facing the truth, for on the same day he told Foreign Secretary Helfferich,

We must not deceive ourselves. We have had successes, but we have not yet had victory. Victory means annihilation of the enemy's power of resistance. When armies of millions of men are opposed, the victor has prisoners. Where are ours? There were some 20,000 taken in the Lorraine fighting, another 10,000 here and perhaps another 10,000 there. Besides, the relatively small number of captured guns shows me that the French have withdrawn in good order and according to plan. The hardest work is still to be done.[14]

His mood "serious and depressed," Moltke now signalled the end of Schlieffen strategy in a general order to all armies:

The enemy has evaded the enveloping attack of the First and Second Armies, and a part of his forces has joined up with those about Paris . . . the attempt to force the whole French army back in a southeasterly direction toward the Swiss frontier is thus rendered impracticable. It is far more probable that the enemy is bringing up new formations and concentrating superior forces in the neighborhood of Paris, to protect the capital and threaten the right flank of the German Army. . . .

Since a decision could only be sought in the center and left,

The First and Second Armies will remain facing the eastern front of Paris, to act offensively against any operations of the enemy from Paris. The First Army will be between the Oise and the Marne, the Second Army between the Marne and the Seine. . . .[15]

Detailed in a General Directive of September 5, these orders meant that Kluck would have to retrace his steps and turn his front from south to west. In turn Bülow would have to turn the Second Army from its southern advance to face west. Hausen's Third Army would continue marching south, but Albrecht's Fourth Army and Wilhelm's Fifth Army would swerve to the southeast. The left-wing armies would continue to try to break through between Toul and Epinal.

Kluck received the new orders early on September 5. Convinced more than ever of Moltke's confusion, he dispatched OHL that his vanguard had contacted the French Fifth Army's left and the BEF, that "the strong forces suspected in Paris are only in the act of assembly" and that it would be a mistake to "invest" Paris before reaching the Seine.[16] He then decided to let his army reach its day's objective *south* of the Marne, but did order one corps to halt where it stood in the north.

This corps, commanded by General von Gronau, had reached its day's objective in the vicinity of Barcy, west of the Ourcq River, when Kluck's order arrived at 1100. Throughout the morning German cavalry had reported increasing French activity to the west, including columns marching on Montgé. Gronau's corps was shy a brigade, while his cavalry division, mauled by the British at Néry, was unable to mount more than two squadrons. He did not relish a fight, but under German infantry doctrine he had to offer one as the best defense. Holding one division in reserve, he now pushed the other to a long wooded ridge running five miles between Penchard and St. Soupplet, an excellent position overlooking the vast plains to the west.

The French columns seen by the German cavalry had been marching since early morning. Part of Maunoury's Sixth Army, they were headed for the Ourcq River, their scheduled line of departure for the new offensive. Far from organized, Maunoury's force comprised two regular divisions, two reserve divisions, a Moroccan brigade of khaki-clad Negroes, a cavalry brigade and an Algerian division.

With no idea that an enemy waited west of the Ourcq— the fault of Sordet's cavalry, now so exhausted as scarcely to

constitute a division—officers led sweating troops along white
*pavé* roads whose bordering poplars shimmered monotonously
in the burning sun.

A few kilometers short of the day's objective, the ridge
now defended by Gronau, the sudden crash of exploding German shells jolted bored *poilus* from their lethargy, jerked
surprised officers into hurling confused orders to deploy in
the flanking flat fields of beet and corn and clover until the
75s rushed up and hastily unlimbered to return the German
fire. By midafternoon long lines of untried reserves and black
colonials snaked across copse-studded fields to begin the slow,
deadly advance to the ridge ahead.

Behind that ridge Gronau was nearly but not quite as
surprised as the French. With the battle joined along the five-
mile front he hastily threw in his single remaining division.
From Penchard on the left to St. Soupplet on the right the
fight continued throughout the afternoon, the French assault-
ing, the Germans defending, then counterattacking.

Although the French outnumbered the Germans—an entire French corps stood uncommitted no more than six miles
away—lack of concerted leadership spelled final French failure. The one French success, the assault on St. Soupplet, soon
yielded to a fierce German counterattack. When darkness
stopped the fighting, Gronau still controlled the vital
ridge.

Well aware of his limited strength, depleted further by
the day's severe casualties, and convinced he was facing an
attack in strength, Gronau sent to Kluck for reinforcement,
then ordered a night withdrawal some six miles east, to the
heights behind the Therouanne valley.

While Galliéni from Paris was reporting "a small successful engagement near St. Soupplet," the outnumbered Germans
were slipping through the darkness unimpeded by the tired
French. Before dawn French patrols approached the villages
so hotly contested the previous afternoon, only to find them

evacuated but for one. In Monthyon wounded German soldiers filled the small church.[17]

Aware by now of Kluck's recalcitrance and frightened more than ever by the reported French build-up in Paris, Moltke sent his Intelligence officer, Lieutenant Colonel Hentsch, to the First Army with a copy of the new Directive. Kluck not only had to receive Hentsch with courtesy, but was forced to listen very carefully to him. Moltke, unlike

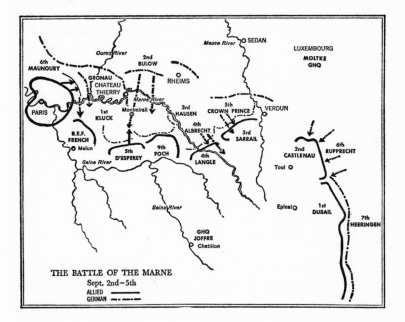

THE BATTLE OF THE MARNE
Sept. 2nd–5th
ALLIED ————
GERMAN ——·——·—

Joffre, rarely employed liaison officers—thus Hentsch, a General Staff officer and member of Moltke's staff, appeared the more important.

On the evening of September 5 Kluck for the first time learned the true state of German affairs. In precise terms Hentsch told him that the general picture looked dubious; all of the "complete victories" reported by the left and center armies had proved no more than local gains. At the moment Rupprecht was suffering severe losses in Lorraine, the Crown Prince and Albrecht were fighting strong resistance everywhere. British troops had landed in Ostend, more were expected. OHL knew for certain that the French were transferring forces to Paris. For all these reasons Kluck had to comply with the retirement order, although the movement "need not be hurried but can be carried out at complete leisure."[18]

Kluck and his chief of staff, Kuhl, agreed and with Hentsch planned the maneuver to take place over the next two days. But now Gronau's report of the day's action reached Kluck—although the fighting proved indecisive, Gronau was falling back to a stronger position, urgently requested reinforcements.

Not at all convinced of a serious attack, Kluck grudgingly ordered Linsingen's corps to march north. The German commander did not know it, but the Battle of the Marne had begun.

# SUNDAY: SEPTEMBER 6

9     THE BATTLE LINE curved from north of Paris down and across the Marne River and south to its tributary the Grand Morin, then east in a wavering line where it climbed to the fortress of Verdun. There it joined at a right angle the Lorraine battle line running south almost to the Alps. On either side of the line for twenty-five miles the impedimenta of fourteen great armies filled the villages and roads, well over two million men, thousands of guns, horses and wagons, ambulances and supply trains—a military concentration never before seen in the world.

The men on the line were mostly veterans now. They knew what it was to march to the sound of cannon, to hear the shells whistling overhead, "making that same revolting noise of some giant dog vomiting."[1] They knew what the cannon did to you inside, that ghastly feeling of impotence against a far-sprung evil, suddenly the *karoomp, karoomp, karoomp* to tear the heart from your company, to foul an honest landscape with entrails of men and horses and twisted broken wagons, and finally if time permitted rude crosses in a field, man's attempt to dignify indignant death.

The Germans outgunned the Allies by far, the big sooty

shells from their heavy artillery being called *marmites* or caldrons by the French, "Jack Johnsons" by the English.[2] The men respected the shells because they were lethal but they no longer feared them, because if you were there you would be killed but if you were forty yards away you would live, and besides many were duds, so you never knew, especially at night. Not so with the 75s, and these the Germans both respected and feared, because they were fast and accurate and lent themselves to a method of firing the French called *rafale*—a squall of shrapnel shells, metal casings that exploded to release iron balls that smothered an area in agony and death. But if the French held the upper hand here, the Germans claimed it back when it came to the machine gun, for this the *poilu* failed to understand; he loathed and feared the dreadful *mitrailleuse* that spit death: you could see it and it mocked you because it was far away and your rifle and bayonet could not reach and when you tried running for it you met death or sometimes wounds.

Wounds were not very nice in 1914. If you were lucky someone finally picked you up, put you on a litter, dumped you at a forward casualty station, a doctor or more likely an orderly poured iodine in the hole and slapped a bandage on it, and there you lay. If the battle went well you might get moved from there, put in a crude, stinking, crowded ambulance wagon that jolted you ten miles back to a church or a barn where you lay in a cloud of flies drinking your blood while tired orderlies tried to make room for the next load. Very often you ate nothing, drank nothing, no one washed you, your bandages went unchanged, many of you died. If the battle went well you might get rescued, dumped in a jolting, crude, stinking ambulance wagon and twelve hours later reach a railhead and then lie in the sun for half a day or a day or two days until the cattle cars chugged in and you were put aboard, and finally were back in some base hospital where charming *mademoiselles* or smiling *Mädchen* tried their best to undo the horror of days.[3]

If you lived, if you survived the shrapnel and the high explosive and the machine gun and the rifle and the bayonet, why then you kept on fighting, attacking or defending, advancing or retreating, eating when you could, sleeping now and again, breathing a reeking foul air of dead and dying cattle and mutilated horses who got in the way of war, a most offensive stench it took some doing to get used to, but after a while you didn't mind it, you stank yourself, you stank so badly a proper staff officer no matter how he tried could not help but wrinkle his nose against your smell and feel glad to regain the rear where a man could wash like a gentleman and eat sitting down and drink wine from a goblet.

Whether you were friend or enemy you thought about wine and baths and violins and love sometimes when you slogged the long, hot roads, watched north blend into south, gray stone give way to red brick and then to stone again in hundreds of little villages, mostly deserted now.

If you were French or English you felt sorry once for the refugees, for pipe-smoking scared men, blue-smocked like their women and children, walking listlessly beside those ridiculous awkward farm wagons pulled by a tired horse or a big dog or humans, piled with a few possessions from a lifetime of hard work. But there were miles and miles, thousands of these wretched people, and soon you began to curse them out of the way as you cursed the loutish French reservists, undisciplined teamsters who jammed the roads with ill-handled wagons and here you were due on those heights or due at that intersection in another two hours and all you could do was stand and hate.

But then you would come on a village where people were hiding and you learned why and your pity returned, for here a few days ago decent people worked hard and lived simply in pursuit of life and suddenly a band of deserters, French deserters, descended and looted and ravaged until the village stood gutted, and you hoped every last one would look at a firing squad, and a few did but many escaped.

There was very great disorder in these days and there would be very great disorder ahead. The German soldier looked ahead to this day, September 6, being like the day before and the day after—forward, always forward, until finally he crushed the enemy as his grandfather had crushed the enemy nearly half a century before. Nowhere along the German line, nowhere at OHL, did the soldier or the officer or the general expect the enemy to attack, no one doubted final victory. To the Allied soldier, to the *poilu* and the Tommy, the day dawned vastly different, dawned with a promise to erase two weeks and 120 miles of humiliating defeat and retreat.

And as these two forces, one determined in its innocence, the other resolute in its anticipation—as these behemoths finally crashed in grand battle the individual melted into terms of armies and corps and divisions, and it is sometimes hard to remember that such ponderous units depend for their being on mere handfuls of soldiers fighting in squads and platoons and sections and batteries and squadrons, and it is hard to remember that five hundred casualties or a thousand or ten thousand mean that many individual humans going to their deaths or suffering in that many different ways, thinking that many different thoughts even though they all stank and wanted food and needed rest. It is very difficult to look at great maps with all those big units neatly positioned and arrows pointing here and there and neat orders of battle and numbered messages and decisions and yet realize that men made this happen.

History is not kind to the soldier because history never smells or eats or relieves itself and even when it does it cannot tell of the hopes of a man if he is dead.

Sunday, September 6: dawn.

North of the Marne River Gronau defended a line running from Puisieux south through Etrépilly and Vareddes, while from below the river a corps was marching to his relief.

To the south Kluck ordered his cavalry on a limited offensive to cover the withdrawal of two corps to the north. A final corps would stay in the vicinity of Esternay until Bülow's Second Army swung into position on Kluck's left.

Bülow's cavalry was planning to penetrate south of the Seine, cut the major railroad line to Paris, then send out extensive reconnaissances to the southwest. Meanwhile Bülow's four corps were to wheel southwest to screen Paris by extending Kluck's left flank.

On Bülow's left one group of Hausen's Third Army was to attack south, one group was to join Albrecht's Fourth Army offensive. The rest of Albrecht's army and the entire Fifth Army were to attack southeast to force the passages of the Moselle and clear the way for the advance of Rupprecht's Sixth Army, now struggling to fight through the Trouée de Charmes between Toul and Epinal.[4]

Thirty-two days of action had markedly changed the strategy and with it the power profile of the German Army. The 3 right-wing armies originally marched with 17 infantry corps; on September 6 they counted 12 corps, a transfer loss of 225,000 troops, plus further severe losses in the numerous encounter battles and from attrition much greater than planned. The boots of men had worn as thin as the shoes of Marwitz' horses and their bodies were as tired. As long ago as Mons the First Army had started to outrun its supply trains. Above and below the Marne some units now were living off the country and sometimes the country did not feed them too well.

The Allied profile had changed as much as the enemy's. While varying factors of battle had influenced Moltke to shift his weight from right to center and left, other factors had caused and were causing Joffre to shift his emphasis in the opposite direction. On August 23 his left wing, consisting of the BEF and the French Fifth Army, counted but 14 infantry divisions and 4 cavalry divisions versus 24 enemy infantry divisions, 5 cavalry divisions and another 5 infantry divisions besieging Namur.

By now, September 6, Joffre had created 2 new left-wing armies, the Sixth and the Ninth, which together with the BEF, the Fifth Army and part of the Fourth Army gave him 41 infantry divisions and 8 plus cavalry divisions with further units coming up from Lorraine. The 3 German right-wing armies now counted 23 plus infantry divisions and 5 cavalry divisions. Obviously Joffre had gained a marked superiority in numbers where once he had been almost fatally inferior.

Joffre's army had been very badly hurt, more so than the German army. But where his enemy was marching away from supply sources, Joffre gained the advantage offered by interior lines of communication: even before the French and British reached the Marne he was pumping men and materiel into his force, simultaneously using a lateral railway complex to change his ratio of strength. He also had relieved those generals he felt unequal to the task in favor of proven fire-eaters desiring a fight. By September 6 he had relieved 2 army commanders, 7 corps commanders, 20 infantry division commanders and 4 cavalry division commanders. Foch and Sarrail now commanded armies, Maud'huy a corps, Pétain a division.[5]

Joffre's position was still precarious.

On the morning of September 6 his offensive lay in the hands of Maunoury's Sixth Army, the BEF and d'Esperey's Fifth Army. But these armies, very tired and still definitely disorganized, stood anywhere from five to fifteen miles behind their scheduled departure lines.

If the Sixth Army were beaten, neither Joffre nor Galliéni cherished any illusions that Paris would hold. Despite Galliéni's most zealous efforts—and for a man of sixty-five years and ill he was remarkably active—the neglect of decades could not be repaired in weeks, a fact sensed by civilian inhabitants whose "mutterings against the leaders of government and army" were already strong enough to be included in the American military attaché's report to Washington.[6]

If his counteroffensive failed, Joffre would fail with it, and so probably would the government, which would leave matters ripe for a growing peace-at-any-price movement among the civilians in Bordeaux and Paris.

Nor were matters too happy to the east, where the rest of the French armies had been ordered to stand on the defensive. Between Foch's Ninth Army and Langle's Fourth Army, the twelve-mile-wide Gap of Mailly was practically undefended, as was the five-mile-wide Gap of Revigny between Langle and Sarrail. Admittedly Joffre had ordered two corps up from Lorraine to plug these vulnerable areas, but these had not yet arrived. The Lorraine front was equally tricky. There Castelnau and Dubail, their armies stripped to the bone, had been fighting furiously since September 4.[7]

In short, on this vital morning Joffre was faced with several questions. Could Maunoury, d'Esperey and Foch, no matter their worth, convert tired armies into the powerful forces needed to carry out their difficult missions? Would Sir John French and the BEF play the vital role asked of them? Would the two corps arrive from Lorraine before the enemy exploited the vulnerable gaps of Mailly and Revigny? Could Castelnau and Dubail hold until a decision had been reached in the west?

These and other problems occupied Joffre's mind, but his recognition of them and his action to overcome them made the counteroffensive a calculated instead of a blind risk. And as he had followed every action of every unit throughout the campaign, so now was he prepared to command the fight before him.

In contrast, control of the situation had begun to slip away from Moltke as early as August 21. Now on September 6, in the schoolhouse at Luxembourg, the old, tired and ill German commander held only dim knowledge of the front. With communications delayed from one to two days and worried about the reported British landing in Ostend, the Russian victory at Lemberg, the failure of Rupprecht's Sixth Army to break through the Trouée de Charmes, Moltke presented the most pitiable of military paradoxes, a commander unable to command.

Early on September 6 Maunoury's Sixth Army crossed the heights so tenaciously defended on the previous day, marched through and around the manure-drenched villages of Penchard and Plessis, St. Soupplet and Monthyon, drab places of gray stone farm buildings and bird-limed slate roofs, then marched in columns down the long slopes and across the plain and past mustard and alfalfa and wheat fields and pretty little red-roofed villages like Marcilly, through rolling country now, with numerous ripe orchards, the woods heavy from Vareddes on the right to Etrépilly and the plateau of Trocy, dangerous country too because ahead of them Gronau's force defended a six-mile line of wooded heights stretching from Vincy south to the Marne.

Even as the *poilus* marched, the early morning air pleasantly cool to tired and dusty faces, the first columns of Linsingen's corps reached the Marne, saw the Moroccans marching in the distance. Linsingen had marched his artillery forward for just this reason and now he opened fire with the heavy 150-mm. howitzers, sent von Trossel's 3rd Division to Vareddes and, sensing the situation, pushed his remaining division north behind Gronau's line while he found the junior commander and relieved him of the battle.

By midmorning French columns were deploying to the attack everywhere along the line. In the south the newly reinforced defenders held their ground, but at the north end of the line Vautier's corps slowly pushed back the outnumbered Germans until Gronau's right was yielding despite the most frantic efforts to hold fast.

Bloody fighting here. Outgunned French batteries had to expose themselves for over a mile while sweating horses struggled through soft fields to bring them within range. The ground was open, German artillery sprayed it, made some direct hits, dug up ground and killed people in digging it. The Moroccans and reserves had tasted war but briefly, it wasn't enough, and they went to the attack without artillery support. This was textbook attack with half the lessons forgotten: sneaking advance using cover and defilade to within six to eight hundred yards of the objective, then the first line up, walking, then trotting, second line up to follow, first line trotting then running, rifles down and bayonets ready and . . . German Maxims concealed and dug in behind wire opening wide up from the dark forest, chopping the first line, com‑ petent gunners throwing in new ammunition belts, the second line running now, a steady light pressure on the hot trigger, the chattering and slow traverse of the water-cooled monster, and the assault died and the men with it.

It was an expensive way to advance, but here and there a battalion did advance. But by the time the French reservists reached Etrépilly there were not many of them left, and by then a fresh German division had reached the north end of the line, met Vautier's corps. The German commander threw his people into a counterattack, pushed back Vautier, shot the reservists out of Etrépilly and, the position restored, went on the defensive, waiting help from Kluck.

That afternoon Kluck learned about the battle, including a report that the British were attacking Vareddes, a conclusion drawn from the khaki uniforms of the French Moroccans and one that very much disturbed the First Army commander, who reported it to OHL as fact. Convinced by a later message that the situation was very serious, Kluck next ordered Arnim's corps to a twenty-five-mile night march north. By 2000 the first German columns were on the road.[8]

The British, whom Kluck had twice destroyed and twice misplaced, began the Battle of the Marne from ten to twenty miles behind the line of departure designated in Joffre's orders. On the left General Pulteney, who had come out on August 30, commanded the new III Corps composed of the

4th Division and the 19th Brigade. In the center stood Smith-Dorrien's II Corps and on the right Haig's I Corps. Early on September 6, its flanks and front covered by cavalry, this force moved out across open, cultivated country dotted with woods and a few forests and split by numerous rivers into one rugged valley after another.

Of the armies at the Marne, the BEF was now in the best condition. Although it had suffered 10 per cent casualties, most of them Smith-Dorrien's, replacements were rapidly filling the ranks, equipment was being issued and, just as important, the blooded troops were eager to move. Of that morning a young subaltern in Haig's corps wrote,

After a good night's rest we had breakfast at 6 A.M. and marched off at 7 A.M. To our surprise and great joy we found we were moving in a northerly direction instead of the usual southerly trek. What a difference it made; it was clear to everyone that we were advancing at last, and a cloud, both mental and physical, seemed to be lifted from us. Yesterday we had plodded along in silence, like men who had an unpleasant job to do, which had to be done, and yet not quite knowing why. Today we seemed to swing along: there was laughter and talking in the ranks. We knew what we were after and meant to get some of our own back.[9]

The left and center corps advanced against almost no opposition throughout the morning, but the cavalry fronting Haig's corps soon struck Marwitz' cavalry coming from the north. By midmorning the British cavalry brigades north of Rozoy were being hit by German artillery and soon retired from their advanced positions on Haig's right. Simultaneously advance elements of Haig's infantry moving on Rozoy found themselves checked. With Smith-Dorrien's corps six miles to his left and the large forest of Crécy to his left front, Haig now halted until the other corps moved in closer to his left as ordered by Sir John French.

Once this maneuver took place, Sir John ordered Haig forward, a delayed message that reached the corps commander too late for him to resume the march. By nightfall his corps stood some eight miles short of its day's objective. Although the other corps reached the Grand Morin River and one battalion of the II Corps crossed it, the BEF still remained ten to twelve miles short of its original departure line.[10]

When Franchet d'Esperey assumed command of the Fifth Army he made it instantly clear that anyone failing to do his duty would be shot. Too experienced a soldier not to recognize the shattered state of his units, however, he ordered his commanders to economize their forces during the advance and he assigned only limited objectives for September 6.

Like the Sixth Army and the BEF, the Fifth Army began the offensive a considerable distance behind the line directed by Joffre. With Conneau's cavalry covering his left, d'Esperey ordered his four corps to attack north in echelon with the right leading. Conneau's cavalry found the way clear on the left and Defforges' X Corps advanced without opposition on the right, but the remaining three corps soon ran into stubborn resistance.

D'Esperey's advance caught Bülow's Second Army in the midst of a wheeling movement which would bring it southwest to echelon on the left and slightly behind the First Army. To aid the maneuver Kluck had left Quast's IX Corps at Esternay while Lochow's III Corps retired north. Hearing an exchange of artillery to the south, Lochow at once halted his retirement. When he learned that Quast was being attacked in strength he wheeled about, deployed on Quast's right and moved to the attack. The two German corps were soon engaged by two French corps intent on gaining the villages of Montceaux and Courgivaux.

Philippe Pétain commanded the left or 6th Division, which was attacking toward Montceaux. Casually sitting a white charger, Pétain brought up his artillery, plastered the German lines with a shrapnel *rafale,* then moved his infantry to the assault. Aloof as ever, the division commander followed the action, cantering here or there as called for. When his lines began to waver he dismounted, walked forward oblivious of the fire, spoke to officers and men, urging them always forward. By evening he held the blazing village of Montceaux, the only commander on the left to take his objective, Mangin having been pushed out of Courgivaux with heavy losses.[11]

Aware of the German strength and not wishing to push his still shaky army too far, d'Esperey early in the afternoon halted his advance with orders to all corps "to very solidly entrench, so that they can resist *coûte que coûte* any enemy counterattack."[12] Like Maunoury and French, d'Esperey found himself considerably short of his initial departure line by nightfall. But with the German infantry and cavalry held on his left—the furthest point south the Germans would reach in the war[13]—and by coming to Foch's aid on the right he had disrupted Bülow's wheeling movement, an accomplishment whose importance would grow with the hours.

Under Joffre's plan the primary mission of Foch's Ninth Army was to protect d'Esperey's right. Foch's front stretched twenty miles from the Brie plateau on his left to the Gap of Mailly on his right. The terrain held by his center greatly strengthened his position. Called the Marshes of St. Gond, it consisted of some twelve miles of a narrow rolling strip of swamp whose few canalized roads were dominated by the heights of Allemant and Mondement on the left and on the center right by Mont Août, a commanding height swelling from the flat country like an ancient burial ground now grown over with shrubs and trees and ideal for artillery emplacements.

Characteristically the fiery Foch converted his defensive mission to the offensive, at least on the left, where he ordered his independent 42nd Division to advance across the plateau north of Sézanne while its neighboring corps pushed advance guards north of the marshes. His remaining corps defended the open, very vulnerable right. To screen the Gap of Mailly, Foch had only a cavalry division, but hoped he could hold until a reinforcing corps arrived from Lorraine.

Bülow's general advance called for his two left-wing corps to reach Sézanne and Marigny-le-Grand, objectives lying deep in Foch's positions. As a result Foch's center and left came early under extremely heavy attacks, and his left, far from advancing, was soon calling for help. The opportune arrival of one of the Fifth Army's corps on the 42nd's left enabled the hard-pressed commander, Grossetti, to cling precariously to positions around La Villeneuve, which he held at the end of the day.

On the right, Foch's greatest worry, half of Hausen's Third Army—three divisions under Kirchbach—advanced cautiously, pushed in Foch's advance guards and forced him back from the Somme. Although Bülow's corps "in spite of every sacrifice, and in spite of heavy losses . . . could gain only a little ground toward the south," by the end of the day's fighting no doubt remained that the entire Ninth Army stood on the defensive.[14]

The advantage gained by Foch's right from Hausen's division of force became Langle's disadvantage. Separated from Foch's army by the Gap of Mailly, Langle's Fourth Army had been ordered to defend a thirty-mile front of rolling country covered with immense woods and numerous drab stone villages.

For the Germans this was part of the decisive sector and a corps order found that day around Vitry and dated September 5 left no doubt of enemy desire:

The object of our long and arduous marches has been achieved. The main French forces, after a protracted retreat, have been forced to accept battle. The great decision is unquestionably at hand. Tomorrow, therefore, the whole German Army, as well as our own corps, will be engaged everywhere on the line Paris–Verdun. To save the welfare and honor of Germany I expect every officer and man, notwithstanding the hard and heroic fighting of these last days, to do his duty unswervingly and to the last breath. Everything depends on the result of tomorrow.[15]

Struck early by half of Hausen's Third Army, fighting with the right wing of Albrecht's Fourth Army toward Vitry, then by the rest of Albrecht's corps along the line, Langle's powerful if tired army defended throughout the day. Although his line temporarily yielded at several points, Langle found his salvation in the terrain that predominantly favored the defender, particularly when exploited with skillful artillery fire.

Earlier in the war French commanders, like the Germans, used artillery in an immediate sense to stop or drive back an attack. But with experience the French, unlike the Germans, began to realize its tremendous destructive power against vulnerable troop concentrations waiting to deploy to the lines.

At the Marne this day and subsequently not only Langle but Foch and Sarrail began to concentrate on this indirect fire. Using shrapnel, the guns fired a combination of *tir fauchant*, a traversing or mowing fire across a target, and of *tir progressif*, a depth fire on an advancing or retreating target. Brave though Langle's infantry was, had it not been for his guns "the result of tomorrow" might well have been a major German breakthrough instead of the stand-off it became on September 6. By nightfall Langle's units were engaged along the entire line, his right fighting furiously to hold until the arrival of Espinasse's reinforcing corps marching from Lorraine.

Langle's position was worsened by Sarrail's Third Army posture on his right. Unlike Foch and Langle, who were ordered to the defensive, Sarrail was to attack Prince Wilhelm's Fifth Army in the flank, the supposition at GQG being that it was advancing south. But Moltke's newest Directive had changed both Albrecht's and Wilhelm's line of advance to the southeast, which meant that Sarrail's attack struck the front of the Fifth Army.

While Sarrail's right and center moved forward in the attack the spearhead of the German advance toward Bar-le-Duc struck the French left, a single corps understrength and desperately tired from the long retreat. In short order the French front caved in, until German soldiers actually rushed one division headquarters and killed the division commander and some of his staff. Although the position was restored by brisk counterattack, the area remained critical, nor did the action in the center and on the right gain ground. Instead of dealing the enemy a mortal blow, by the end of the day Sarrail stood everywhere on the defensive, fighting for his life.

Still, as long as these armies held, Joffre's armies in Lorraine could not be taken in the rear. Of these, Castelnau's Second Army was particularly hard pressed. Faced with heavy siege artillery, Castelnau had warned Joffre on September 5 that he did not know how long he could keep on defending the Grand Couronné of Nancy. Although Rupprecht's army hurled attack after attack against his lines on the 6th, Castelnau did hold and in the afternoon even managed a limited counterattack to restore a position.

But now he was hurt worse than ever and held only slight hope for a prolonged defense. He would have felt better had he known that a corps of Heeringen's Seventh Army already had been summoned to the north, and that opposite him the Sixth Army commander was feeding the most atrocious lies to his troops to keep them in battle. Wrote one German soldier (describing a limited view of the action),

. . . We were ordered to attack. Against us stood a superior power sixfold to ours. On top of all, the battlefield consisted in its greater area of the firing ranges of the Nancy garrison . . . the French artillery knew every distance and consequently was shooting with a dismal precision, and finally, as well, the heavy artillery of the outermost forts of Nancy took part in the fight, whereas we ourselves had only field artillery at our disposal.[16]

Castelnau's troops by now were tired enough. But on September 6 such was the punishment already taken by Rupprecht's soldiers that, in Zola's phrase, they were "terror-stricken at the thought of being still alive."

While everywhere exhausted soldiers slept when they had stopped fighting and stretcher parties probed the blood-soaked ground for wounded, while through the black night resounded the screams of the badly hurt and groans of the nearly dead, while men slept and ate, while ammunition and water and sometimes food was brought to the front, while nervous fingers in forward *picquets* itched around rifle triggers and white flares exploded in the black sky to reveal nothing . . . while this vast battlefield rested uneasily as if burdened by the conscience of its dead, miles away men of consequence made momentous decisions.

To Joffre the day gave a slight tactical edge to the enemy, a strategic edge to himself.

North of Paris Maunoury had failed to advance, but the German reinforcement of a corps was being met by Galliéni, who sent a reservist division from the Paris garrison, and by Maunoury's committing his reserve, the fresh and excellent Algerian Division.

The BEF's advance was disappointing, but it seemed willing to continue, and with Conneau holding the German cavalry perhaps d'Esperey also could advance faster.

Foch was in trouble, but if the XXI Corps closed his right that would help him and Langle. Similarly the arrival of the XV Corps, now quite close, would ease the pressure building between Langle's right and Sarrail's left. If worst came to worst Joffre could abandon Verdun and, if it came to it, Nancy as well. Of course that would raise the very devil with the politicians, and he wouldn't order it without a fight first, but if it were to prove the price of holding the German center and left until he could beat their right then by God he would pay it, and politicians be damned.

Up at Luxembourg the picture was not quite so clear.

Moltke knew by now the decision was at hand, for that afternoon a soldier in the Third Army had found a copy of Joffre's message to the army. Hausen's chief of operations reported its text immediately to OHL, whereupon Moltke notified all army commanders, "According to an order of Joffre's found today, decisive battle has been ordered for today for all the French armies." What the outcome of that battle was he did not yet know, nor did he have any idea of what his commanders were planning for the morrow. He would scarcely have been pleased had he suddenly learned.

Bülow had not yet received Moltke's message when he drew up his next day's orders. Bülow knew that Kluck's two center corps had been moved north, thus creating a gap filled only by two cavalry corps with supporting *Jäger* battalions, a danger brushed off by Kluck since "the repeatedly beaten British will scarcely be quickly induced to come forward and make a powerful offensive."[17] Having been loaned Kluck's two left-wing corps, Bülow decided he should complete his own wheeling movement as quickly as possible, and so ordered the offensive to continue on September 7.

But now Kluck, seriously worried about the battle north of the Marne, ordered *these same two corps* to retire ten to twelve miles behind the Petit Morin River. *This meant that the gap already existing between Bülow's right and Kluck's left would be considerably widened.*

Though greatly surprised and disturbed by Kluck's sudden change of plan, Bülow could do nothing to stop it. Instead, he revised his earlier orders: his left wing would still attack, but on his right one corps was ordered behind the Petit Morin River with a single division of Einem's corps on its right. Apparently afraid for his center, Bülow ordered Einem's other division to remain behind the Second Army in reserve.

At least one of Bülow's generals saw the danger inherent in this order. This was General von Einem, who clearly recognized the precarious weakness of Bülow's right wing—the more so with the loss of Kluck's two corps—and who that night wrote presciently in his diary,

. . . a new Army order: "Thirteenth Division to march on Montmirail. Fourteenth Division to Fromentières as army reserve." What has the Army reserve to do behind the center of the Army? It ought to be on the right wing.[18]

# MONDAY, SEPTEMBER 7

**10** A BIRD FLYING LOW over the long line of battle might have caught something of the panoramic whole, of the enormously varied terrain of ripe wheat fields and orchards and autumnal forests and rolling fields in places covered with crumpled, now bloating figures, of numerous rivers no more than streams for the most part, of long stretches of flat country sprouting woods and forests, of refugees fleeing from a danger not fully understood, the straight roads crowded with trains of ammunition, columns of horse artillery and foot soldiers, of villages burning, their ancient walls shelled to shambles, of men standing by stinking horses, their guns forward firing to shatter the stately poplars, of men everywhere dug into the land or, farther east, firing from immense concrete fortifications, and from this line, this entire line, the acrid smell of rifle and machine gun and artillery clouded with the pervasive stench of the dead and dying.

The fighting continued.

On September 7 men made mistakes, men fought bravely, a few ran, many died, some rested. At times a single soldier influenced an action, at times a regiment, even a corps, made not the slightest difference. An action fought on the right might save the line, one on the left might prove nought, simply cost lives, a needless expenditure of ammunition and energy. One battle might have been important, but time or place or the enemy intervened to sink it into the limbo of dull official history, its commander forgotten, also its dead. One battle might have proved nothing, but time or place or the enemy intervened to raise it to the crucial, never to be forgotten, its commander and its dead memorialized in sweeping cenotaphs of expensive granite.

Then there were the decisions.

A commander might understand a sequence of reports to mean one thing and be right, or one report might not arrive and he would be wrong; with no reports he had to guess, with some he had to estimate—in any case he had to decide, then give orders.

On September 7 the battle was too young for these orders to bring a major decision because strength was too even and where the one commander might reinforce his line the other could check him by reinforcing his line. The battle was not too young to be forming toward a decision, because no battle is, and so it became the more important that the mistakes of subordinate commanders were remedied by their seniors who had also to exploit their gains.

Command is a very complicated affair and the picture obvious to a company commander is never the same picture seen by the division commander, the way the corps commander on the right views the situation invariably differs from the view of his army commander, and so up to the top. This is what is called the chain of command and although it is a butt of many soldier jokes it must be employed if a battle is to gain cohesion. And a battle must have cohesion, it must undergo a controlled growth for it to prove decisive. That is the task of the commander.

South of the Marne and seriously alarmed early on September 7 when he received Moltke's message warning of a general French offensive, Kluck asked Bülow his situation, learned the Second Army was continuing the battle with "so far no decision." Learning next of heavy reinforcements coming out of Paris, Kluck decided to fight his battle on the Ourcq and signaled Bülow: "Participation of III and IX Corps most urgent. Enemy considerably reinforced . . ."[1] Bülow already had withdrawn these two corps and his own X Reserve Corps behind the Petit Morin River when Kluck's imperative message reached him. Disliking to uncover his right flank even further but with no other choice, Bülow now ordered Kluck's two corps to march on the Ourcq.

Here was a decision of paramount importance to the entire battle, a decision made by Kluck and Bülow with no reference to Moltke and with not even a very clear idea of the enemy's intentions. By transferring these two corps north, the German commanders extended a gap already insufficiently guarded by tired cavalry divisions inadequately supported by *Jäger* battalions. Coming up from the south, pointed precisely at this gap, was not only the entire British Army but, on its right, Conneau's cavalry corps and d'Esperey's Fifth Army.

Although Joffre's preponderant strength on the left wing was beginning to make its influence felt, the situation was touch and go on the Ourcq. There fighting resumed with dawn, raged through the day. Despite repeated attacks by the Moroccans and reservists, the German line, strengthened by heavy artillery firing from defilade beyond the range of French 75s, held to the extent that the French began to consider a retirement west. In the center around Etrépilly newly arrived German units joined a counterattack against the French 63rd Reserve Division. Momentarily surprised and confused, the French infantry broke suddenly into retreat.

Now a single soldier emerged to prevent what might have become a disastrous rout. This was Colonel Nivelle, who one day would replace Joffre as commander-in-chief. On the morning of September 7, 1914, he was commanding the 5th

Artillery Detachment. Astride his charger he had been watching the action develop and with horror saw the line begin to crumble. Without hesitating he formed up his 75-mm. horse-drawn batteries, led them forward on the run to the ranks of the retreating infantry. There, ignoring the shot and shell of the enemy assault, he wheeled his guns about, unlimbered and opened direct fire twenty rounds to the minute, a vicious fusillade that broke up the German attack and restored the French line.[2]

Further north the French 14th Division moved out early, their job to push the enemy out of a small village. They fought all day, and many were killed in an action that accomplished little. A survivor described the fighting:

All day long [we] fought at the foot of the Gergogne ravine. We reached the first houses of d'Arcy-en-Multien. Near the cemetery the Germans waited with their machine guns. Around the church and around the bridges across the Gergogne it seemed impossible to pass. The way across the bridge was swept by machine-gun fire—it was a way of death. Our soldiers engaged the enemy one after the other. Their bodies piled up high at the foot of the bridge. Behind this cover our infantry went forward, took cover and fired on the enemy machine guns. The massacre began. A German hidden in a haystack mowed down all our soldiers as they came out of the woods and left the shelter of the trees . . . one of our men had to climb a tree, spy out a sniper and shoot him down. . . .[3]

Further north still, another French division moved out, attacked, then was struck in counterattack by newly arrived units of General von Arnim's corps. The Germans pushed back the French, slowly at first, then suddenly the line folded. The victorious enemy swept forward, but not for long and not for far. The Germans, too, lacked men.

The Germans didn't know it, but the panic-stricken French infantry retreated nearly to Nanteuil. Their error was compounded by Sordet's cavalry which, due to a misunderstanding of orders, also withdrew from the extreme left. Their confusion was understandable—so far the battle of the Ourcq had made little sense to the cavalry. A lieutenant of Dragoons later recalled,

For my part I preserve only a confused and burning recollection of the days of 6th and 7th September . . . the heat was suffocating. The exhausted troopers, covered with a layer of black dust sticking to their sweat, looked like devils. The tired horses, no longer off-saddled, had large open sores on their backs. The heat was burning, thirst intolerable . . . we kept advancing without knowing why or where . . . we knew nothing, and we continued our march as in a dream, under the scorching sun, gnawed by hunger, parched with thirst, and so exhausted by fatigue that I could see my comrades stiffen in the saddle to prevent themselves from falling. . . .[4]

But now, sense or nonsense, for anxious hours the entire French flank stood wide open to an uncomprehending enemy. Then Maunoury learned what had happened, blasted his infantry and cavalry back to the gap which the enemy had not yet exploited. His troubles were scarcely over—he was weak in the north, he knew it, and if the enemy knew. . . .

The enemy did not know, but in Paris Galliéni did. By now this old soldier had become a familiar sight to the people left in the capital, including a thousand American citizens.[5] His eyeglasses perched above a shaggy moustache and wearing black-buttoned boots and yellow leggings below an ill-fitting uniform, Galliéni seemed to be all over Paris, shuffling together the most appalling sort of reserve units to send up to Maunoury.

As usual on September 7 he was working hard, but now he came up with an idea that would perpetuate his name. That afternoon a division which Joffre had transferred from the Third Army detrained in Paris en route to the battle of the Ourcq. And that afternoon, at Galliéni's order, Paris gendarmes flagged down over a thousand taxicabs whose drivers received orders to report at once to the Ministry of War, the Invalides. There before the big brown domed building French officers dispatched convoy after convoy of cabs across Paris, each stopping at various points to collect waiting battalions of two regiments each and proceed to the front, a neat performance that impressed both civilian populace and front-line soldiers with the determination of the French Army and made "Galliéni's taxicabs" a household phrase in the history of war.[6]

Meanwhile in the south Sir John French and Franchet d'Esperey missed the opportunity to turn the gap on their fronts into a tactical victory. The BEF moved out early, not a brisk action. Despite reinforcements and the keen spirit of the men and favorable aviation reports of clear country ahead, the units

moved absurdly slowly, and D. H. [Haig] spent the day going from one Divisional H.Q. to another to try to urge them forward. The cavalry were the worst of all, for they were right behind the infantry. This was gall and wormwood to him, for he had always been first and foremost a cavalry officer.[7]

Where British cavalry fought, they fought hard. An American volunteer driver observed one action at Moncel, and his graphic account is the more interesting because such cavalry actions were soon to vanish from the battlefield:

The 1st Garde Dragoner Regiment of Berlin . . . the proudest, finest cavalry of the German Army—over one hundred of them, seeming double the number to me—were charging across the fields.

On they came, like machine-made waves on a machine-made ocean.

Then from the left shot other horsemen, one well ahead, another not far back, and a scattered scurrying bunch of two score behind, riding like mad, full tilt at the ranks of German pride and might bearing down upon them.

Colonel David Campbell, of the 9th Lancers, close on his heels Captain Reynolds, his adjutant, and forty-five of his gallant regiment were charging more than double their number of the flower of the enemy's horse.

The Germans quickened appreciably, and their lances waved

downwards to the rest. Their pace was slow compared with the whirlwind rush of the smaller band.

I was [sitting] on the wall when the impact came. Crash! went the 9th into the Garde. Colonel Campbell and Captain Reynolds were down, and horses reared and staggered. I wondered that none of the chargers funked it. Each horse seemed imbued with the spirit of his rider. Not one charger "refused.". . .

The 9th scored heavily off their more numerous foes . . . crack British troopers proved their undoubted superiority, man for man, by the number of German dead and wounded we found on the field. Galloping on, the 9th circled round the village and away to the rear. . . .

Strange sights were seen by some of the men in that charge. A non-commissioned officer of the 9th ran his lance full through a German officer who, thus impaled, struck at the lancer and severed his hand at the wrist. One trooper of the 9th ran his lance straight through a German till his hand touched the doomed man's breast. A German horse was seen galloping away with a corpse pinned to its back by a lance. . . .[8]

Aside from this and an action at Faujus where a squadron of British Hussars annihilated a squadron of Guard Dragoons, the British met but slight resistance on September 7. Yet at the end of the day only Pulteney's corps on the left and Gough's cavalry on the right stood at any distance beyond the Grand Morin River. In the center Smith-Dorrien's corps bivouacked in Coulommiers next to the river, Haig's units bedded down south of it—the BEF had advanced but seven to eight miles.

Conneau's cavalry performed with no more dash on the British right. Practically unopposed, this corps ended the day to the right and rear of the BEF. D'Esperey's Fifth Army moved as slowly. Although aware from early morning that the enemy was retreating north his corps advanced with great caution, one waiting while the other fought a rear-guard action, a process that by night found Maud'huy's corps still south of the Grand Morin.

Action increased on d'Esperey's right where German

assaults slammed against Grossetti's independent division and Humbert's Moroccans defending the heights of Mondement. Few people would remember, but the colonial Turcos fought well that day, and if their advance added but little to eventual victory, still it is just such actions that taken together mean eventual victory. Coming up by Soizy-au-Bois, they were hit by 77s firing from some woods on the other side of a mowed hay field. With their own 75s barking back, a regiment deployed in the field began worming its way a half-mile across the sharp, hot stubble while German shells dug graves filled by German Maxims chattering from the trees. When none could have remained alive in that field suddenly with a fearful roar the thin lines rose, lowered bayonets and charged. They lost 50 per cent—but they reached the woods and captured two batteries of 77s.

Off on their right behind the St. Gond marshes French artillery was roaring at the enemy now pushing against Foch's vulnerable right. In late afternoon a violent enemy bombardment struck the French lines. Lasting for two hours, it aroused the suspicions of one Major Jette, chief of staff to General Moussy, commanding the 17th Division behind the marshes. Was the enemy planning a late attack, Jette wondered, or was it a show, a bluff to hide weakness?

Another officer might have confined his curiosity to speculation, and thus saved his own life, but Jette preferred action. He suggested sending a company on reconnaissance across the marshes. Moussy agreed. When enemy fire pushed back the first attempt, Jette persuaded Moussy to let him try with a battalion. Personally leading the columns along the narrow dirt road that split the swampy land, Jette encountered no resistance until he struck the village of Aulnizeux, which he assaulted and captured. But now an alarmed enemy counterattacked in strength. Jette held twice, gave in the third time and ordered a retreat. Personally insuring that his men were clear, he was about to follow when he was killed.[9]

Meanwhile on the right a French battalion fought toward

a small village sited on the curve of the Somme. In the distance behind a hill German howitzers fired on the French lines. The battalion commander hoped to force their position, perhaps capture the guns. His troops had pushed back enemy infantry during the afternoon and now they came on still another enemy line about 100 yards to their front. They could make out the field-gray uniforms stretched along the outside edge of a potato field, firing from behind individual earthworks of potatoes and dirt. Just as the French flexed themselves for an assault the German line rose, started running in retreat. *Eh, bien? C'est bon. En avant. En avant . . .*

Bayonets lowered, the *poilus* rushed into a "charge home" in line. No one noticed a slight disruption of the earth's surface across the road on the left. It was a trench built at right angles to the infanty line and it was covered with boughs and grass and inside it were two Maxim machine guns and their crews.

The Germans waited until the French line stood opposite, then fired, the signal for the "retreating" German infantry to turn about and add to the carnage. The Maxims hit every man but one in the French line. Four days later the bodies were still there—"sixty dead lay in one straight row like the sweep of a mowing machine."[10]

All of these tactical incidents and hundreds more claimed the day of September 7. In Lorraine, where Castelnau was fighting hard against Rupprecht's desperate attacks, a young French lieutenant later recalled, "We were in the clearing, fighting face to face. I had even exchanged three shots from my revolver with a Bavarian officer who had missed me."[11] Hundreds and thousands of soldiers on both sides would recall the "close ones" and those who finally survived would never forget them or any of the sights, sounds and smells of war.

Yet battle was not confined to the front-line soldier. At about the time the young French officer was exchanging "three shots from my revolver with a Bavarian officer," a misunderstanding of orders caused a battalion of French reservists to withdraw from Mont St. Geneviève, a commanding height on the Grand Couronné.

In the confusion the withdrawal became translated by higher headquarters into a rout, and this word went flashing back to Army Headquarters. There the little Castelnau, the lines hard on his aristocratic face, sat in his office listlessly staring at a message—his son had been killed in action. General Anthoine, chief of staff, brought him the news of St. Geneviève. Wearily he nodded—with enemy artillery up there Nancy would be helpless.

Castelnau stood up, told Anthoine to prepare orders for the retreat of the Second Army and to warn the mayor of Nancy that civilian evacuation must begin. Anthoine left the room, but instead of writing the orders he picked up the telephone to GQG.

That afternoon OHL asked Bülow for a situation report. He replied,

The Second Army is engaged in battle with the issue still in doubt on the line of the Petit Morin between Montmirail and Normée.

The 7th [September] at noon the III Corps was sent north of the Marne on the insistent demand of the First Army. The IX Corps is pushing its advance guards toward Chezy. To produce a decisive change it is necessary that it should intervene with important forces.

The British are reported at noon on the 7th from Coulommiers to Choisy, the French from the southwest at Esternay, Sézanne and Fère Champenoise. The cavalry division which was to have been transferred to the Third Army has not yet been sent as it is engaged on the other wing.[12]

With Kluck's two corps transferred from his right, Bülow now committed his single reserve division to his extreme right. But scarcely had he issued the order when his center corps commanders, worried about Jette's assault at Aulnizeux that afternoon, asked him to use the reserve division in their area. Bülow agreed and to protect his weak right withdrew it behind the Petit Morin, thus evacuating Soizy and Oyes—the gains of two days and many men's lives.

While Jette's attack apparently did not alarm Hausen, Foch's incessant artillery fire did. With conventional attacks making slight headway against Foch's right, Hausen turned to the unconventional and ordered his right group of divisions to a pre-dawn surprise attack for the next day.

Five years before the Battle of the Marne Count Alfred von Schlieffen described the modern commander's headquarters during battle:

The modern commander-in-chief is no Napoleon who stands with his brilliant suite on a hill. Even with the best binoculars he would be unlikely to see much, and his white horse would be an easy target for innumerable batteries. The commander is farther to the rear in a house with roomy offices, where telegraph and wireless, telephone and signaling instruments are at hand, while a fleet of automobiles and motorcycles, ready for the longest trips, wait for orders. Here, in a comfortable chair before a large table, the modern Alexander overlooks the whole battlefield on a map. From here he telephones inspiring words, and here he receives the reports from army and corps commanders and from balloons and dirigibles which observe the enemy's movements and detect his positions.[13]

In Luxembourg Helmuth von Moltke was certainly "farther to the rear," but that is about as far as the comparison goes. Already on September 5 Falkenhayn noted, ". . . Only one thing is certain: our General Staff has completely lost its head. Schlieffen's notes do not help any further and so Moltke's wits come to an end."[14]

On September 7 Moltke received but one report from Bülow and one from his commander at Maubeuge that the fortress had finally surrendered. Instead of inspiring words to his commanders, much less orders, Moltke maintained com-

plete silence, his frame of mind well illustrated by a letter of
September 7 to his wife:

Today destiny will deliver a great decision. Since yesterday the
whole German Army from Paris to Upper Alsace is at grips with
the enemy. If I could give my life to achieve victory, I should
do it with infinite joy, following the example of thousands of our
brothers who have already fallen. What torrents of blood have
flowed! Into what incalculable despair innumerable innocent
people have been plunged whose houses and farms have been
burned and devastated! I shudder sometimes at the thought; I
have the impression that I am responsible for all these horrors,
and yet I could not do otherwise.[15]

One of the many ironies found in the Battle of the Marne
was the resemblance between the command installation fore-
seen by Schlieffen and the actual French GQG. Located now at
Châtillon-sur-Seine, about 150 miles southeast of Paris and 70
miles south of Foch's front, GQG operated in an old convent
ringed with barbed wire and amply guarded by troops.
Very few persons in France knew the location of this headquarters, and those who did visit it held special passes and
were escorted under guard. There they found the fleet of
motorcars and motorcycles used by Joffre's numerous liaison
officers, a complete communications system that functioned
amazingly well and batteries of typists pounding out the stack
of orders necessary to run a vast army.[16]

In his personal office, a converted monk's cell, the stout,
sloppily uniformed commander-in-chief worked hard on September 7. Fearing that d'Esperey's delay would hold back the
BEF, he early had the Fifth Army commander telephoned—it
was important that d'Esperey bring his left up to the BEF's
right.

Deciding to streamline communications with the Sixth
Army, he sent off a dispatch to Galliéni—henceforth Joffre
would send orders directly to the Sixth Army commander, a
copy to Paris.

As the situation built up from morning air and cavalry reports he discussed it with his principal staff officers, heard them out and in the afternoon sent General Instructions Number Seven to his left wing: Maunoury to cease his costly and futile frontal attacks in favor of attacking the northern flank; the BEF to push north of the Marne as fast as possible; the Fifth Army to push its left wing forward while supporting Foch with its right.

A message from Sarrail had come in early that morning. Sarrail was worried about his left—wanted more support from Langle. The Third Army commander couldn't seem to understand that Langle had enough problems with *his* left without having to worry unduly about his right. Joffre reminded Sarrail of this, but to help him out ordered Castelnau to send up a cavalry division for the Third Army's right. Another message came from Sarrail indicating he must at all cost keep his right firmly wedded to Verdun. Joffre could not agree—although Prince Wilhelm's Fifth Army stood spread-eagled on either side, Verdun was a first-class fortress protected by a powerful mobile garrison defending from a network of trenches and outside forts. More sharply Joffre dispatched Sarrail in the afternoon,

I authorize you, if you judge it expedient, to withdraw your right [that is, away from Verdun] so as to cover your communications and to lend power to the action of your left wing. It is important not to allow yourself to be cut off from the Fourth Army.[17]

This matter had been no sooner attended to than General Anthoine called from the Second Army to report Castelnau's personal catastrophe and his major decision to withdraw. Joffre instantly got Castelnau on the telephone, listened politely to his grave recital of doom.

"If I try to hold where I am," Castelnau concluded, "I feel that my army will be lost. We have got to face the idea of immediately retreating behind the Meurthe [River]."

"Do nothing of the kind," Joffre told him. "Wait twenty-four hours. You do not know how things are going with the enemy. He is probably no better off than you are. You must not abandon the Grand Couronné and I give you formal orders to hold on to your present positions."[18]

With that he sent an aide to confirm his verbal orders and instruct Castelnau to "hold on in front of Nancy at any cost."

As was his daily wont, Joffre walked for two miles that evening. He probably had not yet heard of Nivelle's action at Etrépilly that day, nor of the brave charge of the Turcos, probably not of Jette's death or of the ambush of Foch's battalion. He certainly held no idea of Hausen's plan for a pre-dawn attack against Foch's fragile right. Nor could he know what results he had achieved during the day or how his orders affected the enemy or that the reserve battalion on Castelnau's front even now had reoccupied Mont St. Geneviève and the position was secure.

Joffre had a lot to worry about on the night of September 7, but he had spent the day trying to come to grips with his problems, trying to give his army a cohesion that in turn made some sense out of Nivelle's stand and the charge of the Turcos and the brave unknown or unseen private soldier who had stood his small piece of ground in the face of the enemy, and perhaps had died doing it.

# TUESDAY: SEPTEMBER 8

**11** A MESSAGE from Kluck sent the previous afternoon reached OHL early on September 8:

Following the arrival of the IV Army Corps on the right wing, the action of the II and IV Reserve Corps progressed on the line east of Nanteuil–Meaux. The III and IX Corps are on the march toward the battlefield [of the Ourcq]. The attack will be continued tomorrow with prospects of success. The Cavalry Corps is covering the front from Meaux to Coulommiers, where no important enemy force has advanced. The enemy has been using a great quantity of heavy artillery probably brought from Paris. Enemy: British forces and it seems the V and the VII French Army Corps.[1]

What Kluck called the British forces in reality were the Moroccans, a careless mistake that further distorted OHL's estimate of enemy strength and positions.

A message from Bülow, also sent on the 7th, next arrived: the Second Army had held its positions and its left was attacking with Hausen's right early on the 8th, but "because of heavy losses" it had "only the combat strength of three army corps."[2]

OHL next intercepted a disquieting message from Richtofen, commanding the I Cavalry Corps, to Marwitz on his right: Richtofen's defensive line on the Petit Morin River was broken and he was retiring slowly north behind the Dolloir River.

Convinced finally that a dangerous gap existed between the First and Second Armies—the same gap that had been developing since September 6—Moltke ordered units from his Antwerp force and from a corps now freed by the fall of Maubeuge to march immediately on St. Quentin. He then called a meeting of his staff, who seem to have held no clearer idea of the actual situation than he did. Apathetic to the point of oblivion, he found little encouragement from von Stein, his deputy, who said "we must not lose our heads" but did nothing.

Eventually someone suggested sending Lieutenant Colonel Hentsch to visit the front and determine the true situation, and Moltke agreed. Hentsch was the General Staff officer who a few days earlier had visited Kluck. Experienced and able, he had known Kluck and Bülow before the war, and Moltke apparently felt no compunction about giving him enormously important orders.

These were oral orders and they were to cause unending controversy, but persons who have made a close study of what was to become known as "the Hentsch case" more or less agree as to the content: if one of the right-wing armies was retreating, Moltke allegedly told him, Hentsch should try to influence the movement so as to close the gap between these armies, that is the First Army should withdraw to the line Soissons–Fismes, the Second Army to a line behind the Vesle River.[3]

The situation which Hentsch was to report already had changed when he left Luxembourg about 1100 and it continued to change while he sat in his staff car en route to his first stop, Fifth Army Headquarters.

Far to the west Maunoury received new orders from Joffre, who early in the day learned that his garrison of

30,000 men had finally surrendered Maubeuge, besieged since August 24. Realizing this would free at least one German corps, besides opening a vital railway line, Joffre ordered Maunoury to march his cavalry northeast to cut Kluck's communications.

With Joffre's approval, Maunoury had relieved Sordet, but the new corps commander, Bridoux, could only furnish one division, so exhausted was the corps. With this on the march, Maunoury tried to carry out Joffre's orders to outflank the German right by pushing a fresh infantry division to the north of his line, where it joined in attack with the worn 61st Division. Although regaining the ground lost the previous evening, the French attack soon slowed against the entrenched positions even as the first units of Lochow's corps began trickling into the German line.

A French assault against the German center fared little better but did cause Kluck to strengthen this area at the expense of the north. At the same time he responded to sinister aviation and cavalry reports of enemy advances in the south by ordering two infantry brigades and two regiments of field artillery to defend the north bank of the Marne. Having decided to throw what remained of his newly arrived corps into an all-out attack in the north the next day, Kluck then drove north to co-ordinate this move.

By now what was left of Bridoux' cavalry was on the march, with the troopers of the 22nd Dragoons sitting up "in their saddles, forgetting their fatigue and hunger." They already had enjoyed good luck when

. . . a young dragoon, sent forward as scout, penetrated into a farm and there found fifteen Prussian staff officers engaged in stuffing themselves with food. He calmly pointed his revolver at them and advised them to surrender. "My regiment will be here directly; any resistance is useless." In reality he had to keep them under the muzzle of his revolver for a long quarter of an hour, for the regiment was still far off. A major having shown signs of moving, the dragoon blew out his brains at point-blank range, and he succeeded in keeping the rest terrorized until our arrival. This capture stimulated still further the general good humor. . . .

The day's action nearly progressed into a fabulous *coup* because later,

. . . three German motor cars were sighted 300 meters off, going at a prudent pace. At once the ranks were broken and we galloped furiously at them, each straining hard to be the first to get there; but by quickly reversing their engines they succeeded in turning and made off at top speed. . . .[4]

Inside one of the automobiles was General von Kluck, commanding the First Army.

Meanwhile from early in the day Kluck's own cavalry had its hands full south of the Marne. At 0400 the BEF moved out toward the Petit Morin River. According to an observer,

We were treated to a wonderful sunrise. As we started . . . the sky along the eastern horizon showed salmon pink to palest blue. The fields by the roadside were full of cavalry units and batteries of guns. Regiments advancing over the meadows in line of squadrons, an imposing array; batteries, belated, galloping into position with an inspiring rattle and bang over any and all obstructions; motorcycles dodging and panting past less swift users of the road; and even the push-bicyclists putting every ounce of energy into their pedalling—it was good to be alive that morning as the salmon in the east changed to pale gold and the blue to turquoise.[5]

British horse soon struck strong cavalry rear guards supported by emplaced *Jäger* battalions on both sides of the stream. As infantry and artillery closed from behind, cavalry skirmishes turned into a series of waspish firefights while the British Tommies worked their way slowly across the heavily wooded, defended valley to the river. On the extreme left of the British line Pulteney's III Corps stood before La Ferté-sous-Jouarre, helplessly watching units of Lochow's corps marching north across the bridges—out of range of British artillery.

Joffre's new orders changed d'Esperey's advance slightly to the northeast. While Conneau's cavalry worked up to the Petit Morin and crossed it after a British brigade cleared the heights, the infantry moved more slowly. Delayed nearly two hours in starting, Maud'huy's march on the left bogged down further when his columns intermingled with those of his neighboring corps. Although his front was clear, a report of German artillery positions west of Marchais-en-Brie caused him further delay; in turn, the two corps on his right halted.

D'Esperey's right corps spent the morning defending against the same attack faced by Foch's left, but before that action developed Foch's right found itself in serious trouble. At 0300 Hausen's surprise attack, undertaken in conjunction with Bülow's left, fell on the French lines, pushed in the outposts and pressed on to tumble all three French divisions back onto the reserve 18th, a disastrous confusion that gave the enemy the key village of Fère Champenoise. By midmorning, however, some of the French units regained sufficient cohesion to stand against the enemy in a dozen places while a fierce artillery duel pulverized the village and turned the flat country into a piece of hell.[6]

On Foch's right Albrecht continued his attack against Langle's left, but now the long-awaited XXI Corps was rapidly approaching from the south. Similarly, Sarrail met Wilhelm's renewed assaults with his shaky left buttressed by the newly arrived XV Corps. On his right the VI Corps, its artillery directed by aerial observers, unleashed a murderous fire against the Crown Prince's center.

Frustrated at the failure of his frontal attacks, Wilhelm now decided to try a flank attack against the four little forts guarding the line of the Meuse between Verdun and Toul. That morning units of the German V Corps advanced west against the second of these. This was the fort of Troyon. It was defended by one infantry company and some twelve guns under Commandant Toussaint, and it was backed by a cavalry division busy blowing the bridges to its rear.

About noon Lieutenant Colonel Hentsch arrived at Prince Wilhelm's headquarters, seemed satisfied with the Crown Prince's progress and went on to Fourth Army Headquarters, where Duke Albrecht briefed him. From there he telephoned Luxembourg, reported favorably to his colleague, Lieutenant Colonel Tappen of Operations. Traveling on to the Third Army, he talked briefly to Hausen, was impressed with the results of the pre-dawn surprise attack and dispatched Moltke, "Situation and point of view entirely favorable at the Third Army."

While Hentsch was being driven to Second Army Headquarters, the battle continued. North of the Marne Maunoury's attempt to outflank the German right ended in early afternoon when a newly arrived division again bolstered the German line. No more did the French succeed in the center. Although the enemy abandoned Etrépilly he maintained his line on the heights behind, his defiladed heavy artillery taking a dreadful toll of the attacker. But in the south the enemy at last yielded Vareddes to the persistent Moroccans and pulled his last rear guards back across the Marne.

Although tired, in some cases exhausted, the German soldier refused to panic here or elsewhere on the battlefield. When he attacked it was in good order, and when he retreated it was in good order. This was an impressive display of training, enough so that one of his own fighting on the Ourcq impassionedly noted,

Every German soldier killed in action died with his knapsack on, as if he had prepared himself for a parade of the dead. When he fell he displaced nothing: his belt, his cartridge boxes, his tassel, bayonet and spade, tent-square, the rolled-up greatcoat . . . everything at its proper place, folded up and buckled and tied fast . . . not even the helmet with its cover rolled away or came off the head. Even when he was killed, it was according to regulation.[7]

With the end of the day's indecisive fighting Maunoury and Galliéni held pessimistic views about their position. So far three and a half days of intensive attacks had not budged the Germans except when they desired to withdraw. French attacks against entrenched lines in the south and center left the Barcy plateau a virtual above-ground cemetery, while German trenches near Etrépilly, struck repeatedly by French artillery, looked like vast charnel houses with "flocks of crows hovering over the woods revealing where other corpses lay." Now with German reinforcements closing, the Sixth Army would have a problem in holding, much less resuming the offensive.

That afternoon at Maunoury's headquarters the two generals agreed that the Sixth Army must go on the defensive until the BEF moved onto Kluck's flank and rear. In the evening Maunoury dispatched Joffre:

I have all my forces engaged . . . my enveloping maneuver to the north is no longer possible by reason of the extension of the enemy's front as far as Thury and the wood 3 kilometers east of Cuvergnon. . . . I am resisting on my positions. If too sharply attacked, I shall refuse my left little by little, in such a way as to march later toward the north when the pressure against me has been relieved by the offensive of the British and the Fifth Army. Have taken two flags and numerous prisoners; heavy losses.[8]

Maunoury's fears for the morrow were being fully justified at Kluck's headquarters. Strengthened now by the two corps from the south and a brigade from Brussels which arrived north of Nanteuil, Kluck ordered an attack in the north for early on September 9 and so informed OHL, adding that he was defending the line of the Marne with cavalry and a composite brigade against an attack forming from Coulommiers.[9]

This attack referred to the BEF's slow but steady advance

of the afternoon. Urged on by no less than three messages from Joffre, Haig's divisions by 1400 had opened the bridges across the Petit Morin to Allenby's cavalry, which quickly crossed and fanned out patrols to the north. Continued stiff resistance in the center delayed the crossing there for another hour, but by evening Sir John's right and center corps were marching to the Marne while his left corps stood south of the river dropping 60-pdr. high-explosive shells into enemy units on the other side.

The day's fighting, which cost the British about 600 casualties, infused the troops with new spirit. In the first serious engagement since Le Cateau they had fought their way through terrain that offered every advantage to the defender, had pushed the enemy back, given him 500 some casualties and captured another 500. Unfortunately the very sultry weather now turned into a thunderstorm and a cloudburst ended operations.[10]

Meanwhile d'Esperey's left moved more slowly in its advance on the key village of Montmirail. Although frontal attacks by two corps in the afternoon failed to take the village, units of Maud'huy's corps on the extreme left forced the Petit Morin River and planned to strike the German flank during the night.

But now Foch's problems had doubled. At noon a German division debouching from the St. Gond marshes fell on Foch's center corps. Although fast and accurate 75-mm. artillery fire from Mont Août saved the line, the enemy now stood south of the marshes, his line tied into the penetration severely pushing against Foch's right.

Refusing to be beaten, Foch spent the day

bursting like a whirlwind into every headquarters, his face contracted, his body all tense and contracted, gesticulating, fulminating in jerky ejaculations.

To a general in agony who tells him: "My troops are yielding under superior numbers. If I do not get reinforcements, I cannot answer for anything!" he replies with a sweeping and furious gesture:

"Attack!"

"But. . . ," says the general.

"Attack!"

"But . . ."

"Attack, attack, attack!" bellows Foch, who dashes out charged like an electric battery, with fierce energy and unconscious aggressiveness, rushing elsewhere to harden other energies, to toughen other faltering wills.[11]

There were plenty to toughen. The day's vicious fighting left the Ninth Army in terrible shape. Every battalion Foch owned was engaged, dead and wounded filled the field, very brave men desperately held pockets of resistance while those officers left alive tried to reorganize shattered and confused units.

Foch first asked Langle for help, a futile request since Langle's left stood too far east to be of use except by attacking from its present location. He had better luck with d'Esperey. Deciding that Foch's need must come before his own general advance, the Fifth Army commander released a corps to him for the next day.

Langle's own situation improved immeasurably during the afternoon, thanks to the arrival of units of the long-awaited XXI Corps. Although too late to influence the day's fighting, the fresh troops completely altered Langle's position. That night he told Joffre he would counterattack on the 9th— that morale was now excellent.

Sarrail, too, held during the afternoon while on his right the VI Corps artillery pounded the batteries of the enemy to destruction. To aid the little fort of Troyon, Joffre ordered Castelnau to send up another cavalry division and an infantry brigade from the Toul fortress.

Castelnau and Dubail did not know it but their worries were nearly over. The same conference that decided Moltke to send Hentsch to the front caused him to send Major Roeder of Operations to Rupprecht's Sixth Army Headquarters. Rupprecht was not there, so Roeder delivered Moltke's orders to the chief of staff: the Sixth Army would break off its offensive and prepare to withdraw toward the frontier for transfer to the west.

Hentsch arrived at Second Army Headquarters late in the evening. Instead of the coldly arrogant, supremely self-confident Prussian commander familiar to every officer in the German General Staff, Bülow was now a tired and very worried old man whose mind had not been relieved by a day spent at the front.

His exact situation was brought out in a conference with Hentsch that was attended also by von Lauenstein, chief of staff, who was ill, and Lieutenant Colonel Matthes, chief of operations. Bülow explained that the Second Army's problem had begun when Kluck recalled the III and IX Corps from Bülow's right. Ever since, Bülow had been racing against time, trying to wrest victory with his left in conjunction with Hausen's Third Army while his right held.

His right was now very weak. Early that day his cavalry had fallen back before the advancing enemy. Throughout the day his aviators confirmed the advance of long enemy columns. That afternoon the enemy had struck him hard where he was weakest—now only one brigade formed the flimsiest defense on the extreme right around Marchais-en-Brie.

"As a result of all that we have been through and of the hard combats of the last few days," Bülow told Hentsch, "the Second Army has naturally lost a considerable part of its combat value. It is no longer capable of forcing a decisive victory. As a result of the transfer of two army corps from the left to the right wing of the First Army, a gap has been created which forms an immediate danger to the inner wings of both the First and Second Armies. I am informed that enemy columns, brigades or divisions, are on the march into this breach, and I have no reserves left to attack the enemy or to hold him off.

"The enemy has two alternative courses open to him, either

to turn against the left wing of the First Army or to march
against the right wing of the Second Army. Because of our lack
of reserves, either movement might lead to a catastrophe. If the
enemy compels a retreat by force of arms, the withdrawal would
have to be made through a hostile country and the consequences
to this Army might be incalculable. It should therefore be considered whether it would not be better, viewing the situation
as a whole, to avert the danger by a voluntary concentric retreat
of the First and Second Armies."[12]

While Bülow was talking, d'Esperey's left-wing division,
now across the Petit Morin, had fought for and won control
of the Courmont woods west of Marchais-en-Brie. After
waiting out the same storm that had disrupted the British
advance, French 75s roared in the night while infantry pushed
forward in bayonet assault to take trenches and outposts
defending the village. The assault cost the French 400 casualties
but they found the German trenches "stuffed" with dead and
wounded, and when patrols entered the village it was empty.[13]

This was a victory of immense importance. Einem,
commanding the VII Corps, at once telephoned Army Headquarters and reported the loss. Bülow recognized the import of
the defeat. With Marchais-en-Brie in the hands of the French,
Montmirail was no longer defensible. Bülow now ordered his
right-wing commanders to begin withdrawing to a line some
six miles east, which once more widened the gap between
the two armies.

The conference then resumed, its principal point being
the breach between Kluck and Bülow. If it could not be
closed, Bülow thought he would have to retire behind the
Marne.

Sometime after midnight Bülow ended the meeting. In
nine words Hentsch summed up the results to OHL: "Situation
of the Second Army serious, but not hopeless."

Having issued no orders to his armies for two days, Moltke
continued to maintain his uninformed aloofness during the

vital day of September 8. Except for the little snippets now and again tossed at him by Hentsch, the German commander-in-chief held only a slight notion of developing events, and apparently no notion of personally interceding to influence them.

In almost fantastic contrast, Joffre followed each action with the keenest interest. Pinning his hopes on Maunoury's offensive, he authorized the Sixth Army commander to transfer a division sitting idly south of the Marne to the battle line. During the day he rained messages on Sir John French urging him to debouch across the Marne. That night he again authorized Sarrail to withdraw his right from Verdun if necessary to give greater power to his left.

His hopes of Maunoury's success dashed by the day's action, Joffre now sought to exploit the developing situation in the center. At 1900 on September 8, Special Orders Number Nineteen directed Maunoury to hold fast on September 9, avoiding all decisive action and if necessary withdrawing his left toward the Entrenched Camp of Paris. The British Army was to cross the Marne and attack the left and rear of Kluck's army. The Fifth Army, its left covering the British and its right supporting Foch, would advance its center to drive the enemy across the Marne.[14]

Despite Foch's folded right Joffre felt pleased with the situation on the night of September 8. He did not know it, but events were shaping fast. The fog of war was lifting—the decisive day was at hand.

# WEDNESDAY: SEPTEMBER 9

**12**  AT SECOND ARMY Headquarters early in the morning Lieutenant Colonel Hentsch met a second time with Lauenstein, Bülow's chief of staff, and Matthes, his chief of operations. Bülow himself was absent and the meeting seems to have been a rehash of the earlier one.[1]

Seen in the light of dawn shaded by the night's ominous reports, the Second Army's profile loomed as dangerous to the three officers. Unless Kluck's First Army withdrew east to close the gap existing between it and the Second Army, the latter's right undoubtedly would be turned. But for the First Army to break off the action and withdraw in time to close the gap was probably impossible. To be safe, the Second Army must withdraw behind the Marne, then the Vesle River.

Moltke had instructed Hentsch that if one of the right-wing armies was retreating he should try to direct the movement so as to close the breach. With Lauenstein's statement that the Second Army must withdraw—a statement made with the enormous authority of the chief of staff's position and probably with the knowledge of Bülow's own mind—Moltke's first condition was met. According to his orders, Hentsch should now try to influence the movement so as to close the gap. In short, he must try to persuade Kluck to withdraw toward the line Soissons–Fismes.

Without again seeing Bülow, Hentsch left for Kluck's headquarters.

Meanwhile cannons roared the continuing battle of the Ourcq. For the French Sixth Army, the job that day was to hold until the BEF crossed the Marne to fall on Kluck's flank and rear. If the army broke, its units were to retire south on the Entrenched Camp of Paris where Galliéni, alive to the situation, had scratched up a second line of defense consisting of garrison troops brought out from Paris.

Kluck also had to hold. While his divisions in the south stood their positions and while his cavalry-infantry force held the line of the Marne against the BEF, he would attack in the north, a three-pronged effort spearheaded by Quast's newly arrived units.

But Quast's people were tired. They had marched two days to the battle, their boots were nearly worn through and their units weakened from the long campaign. Captain Bloem's battalion was reduced to two composite companies and others were in worse condition:

A captain, wandering aimlessly and alone, spoke to me [Bloem recalled]: his speech was confused and the light of my torch showed a haggard face with the restless shifting eyes of a madman: "I once had a company. I'm all that's left of it."[2]

Fatigue and hunger had worked their enervating rules until "one's mind, heart and soul were consumed away; a great vast melancholy and misery hung over us all, seemingly over the whole world."[3] The attacking divisions had arrived only on the previous afternoon, units were mixed, and now while Quast desperately was trying to ready them for the offense the morning wore away.

It was a dangerous delay because early that day bugles sounded in British bivouacs. By 0500, before Hentsch had risen, British cavalry had saddled up, were on the march. A half-hour later British Dragoons and Hussars rode over the bridges of the Marne, fanned out to cover the infantry behind them.

Soon after 0800 Sir John's right claimed the heights north of the Marne. In the BEF center Smith-Dorrien's corps found the bridges intact (the German brigade there had no engineers, could not blow them), crossed over, the leading units some two miles north in the early morning. But on the left Pulteney's corps stopped, for there the bridges were blown and German artillery fired from the northern slopes. Brigade columns approaching the twisted bridges of the 80–90-yard-wide river met fire from machine guns skillfully hidden in buildings on the other side. They stopped, then fell back to wait for the barrel-chested draft horses to snort up with the big five-ton 60-pdrs.

On the British right d'Esperey's Fifth Army marched early, its commander's orders to run over enemy rear guards which "should be crushed by violent artillery fire, turned by infantry and pursued by cavalry." With Conneau's horse marching on the left the ponderous army moved out. Although some units gained their initial objectives by 0800 and general resistance confined itself to local rearguard actions, the fatigue of days quickly told and progress slowed toward the distant Marne, despite the most violent efforts of the frantic d'Esperey.

On d'Esperey's right Foch from the break of dawn faced a situation as grim as Maunoury's in the north. Shielded by heavy mist a German battalion had sneaked up the slopes of Mondement toward Moroccan outposts who had been warned by their commander, "The Germans are bottled up and Mondement is the cork; we must never let it go."

But by September 9 the fierce Moroccans had been fighting long and hard. One colonial regiment was down to 900 out of 3,000 men; some units had not eaten hot food since September 5, some received neither food nor ammunition on September 8. Struck now by a surprise blow from the tangled, misty slopes they gave way, recovered only to find the enemy defending behind the thick walls of the Château de Mondement that stood imposingly amidst shade trees atop the height.[4] Simultaneously Bülow's left and Hausen's right opened a murderous barrage against Foch's battered right, followed it with infantry assault that swept across the seven-mile front to hurl the French back another mile or two and to put German units halfway up the slopes of vital Mont Août.

Dawn also brought fighting to the east. Although Langle pushed his fresh corps to the attack on his left, his right remained hard-pressed under the combined and now desperate attack of two German armies. Sarrail, too, had his hands full. On his left the full effect of his newly arrived corps was not yet felt. On his right rear only a meager force stood on the Meuse behind the little fort of Troyon which that morning defiantly refused to surrender although in twenty-four hours over 400 heavy shells landed to put seven of its guns out of action.[5]

Events moved rapidly now.

On the eastern front Prince Rupprecht returned to Sixth Army Headquarters, listened unbelievingly to the fantastic terms of Moltke's order. Furiously he telephoned Luxembourg. Lieutenant Colonel Tappen of OHL took the call: no, there was no mistake, the Sixth Army's offensive was finished.

At what must have been about the same time, Bülow heard Lauenstein's report of the earlier conference with Hentsch. He later wrote,

When early on September 9 several enemy columns crossed the Marne . . . the retreat of the First Army became inevitable, in view of the tactical and general situation, and the Second Army had to fall back if its right flank were not to be enveloped. . . .[6]

Without determining Kluck's actual situation, without consulting Moltke or even sending him the same message, Bülow now dispatched Kluck and Hausen,

Aviators report advance of four long columns over the Marne. Heads at 8 A.M. at Nanteuil, Citry, Pavant, Nogent. Second Army begins retirement, right flank Damery.[7]

While Bülow's vital message was being enciphered for transmission, Lieutenant Colonel Hentsch sat hunched in his staff car. For miles it had inched along roads jammed with troops, horse-drawn artillery, cavalry patrols, long supply and ammunition trains, dozens of ambulances—*all moving east.*

To the staff officer undergoing his first war, the confused picture of withdrawal must have suggested disorderly retreat and with it impending disaster, an impression undoubtedly heightened when he was warned to detour north because of enemy cavalry ahead.

The picture was fairly accurate. At Mareuil, First Army Headquarters and Hentsch's destination, Kluck learned of "strong enemy infantry and artillery at Charly over Marne bridge." When further reports confirmed the presence in force of the BEF, Kluck faced a dangerous situation. On his right Quast had not yet begun his attack, but now an enemy attack obviously was building against his weak left. To gain time he ordered his left and center pulled back to a line *facing south instead of west.*

This movement was well under way, as was Quast's attack in the north, when shortly before noon Hentsch arrived at Mareuil. Reporting to Kuhl, Kluck's chief of staff, Hentsch quickly explained the bleak situation at the Second Army. His pessimism was soon rewarded by the arrival of Bülow's message that "Second Army begins retirement."

Satisfied that even if Kluck rolled up Maunoury's left he was in no condition to exploit the victory, Hentsch now repeated Moltke's instructions for the First Army to withdraw to the line Soissons–Fismes where its left would join Bülow's right. Although Kluck was not present and Hentsch left before he returned, the First Army commander agreed with the decision:

. . . on the grounds of the now fully changed condition of affairs, the army commander—bearing in mind the seriousness of his decision—decided on an immediate commencement of the retirement in a northern direction.[8]

Hentsch did not immediately notify Moltke of this event, so OHL remained almost wholly in the dark until intercepted messages confirmed the beginning of Bülow's retirement.

Convinced now that a general retreat was necessary—to add to his troubles, the Belgian Army was starting another sortie from Antwerp—Moltke went to the Emperor, who forbade any such action until more complete reports arrived from the right wing.

While Hentsch and Kuhl had been conferring at Mareuil, Bülow's retirement message reached Hausen's headquarters. With his own battle running smoothly Hausen could not understand Bülow's decision and indeed doubted the message until a subordinate commander reported an order from Bülow to break off the action. With the Second Army's retirement a confirmed fact, Hausen decided he must withdraw his own right wing. For the time he would not disturb his left.

By midafternoon on September 9 the force primarily responsible for this incredible series of German command decisions—the BEF—stood halted. Alarmed at aviation reports of heavy German forces north of Château-Thierry, Haig held up his corps until the French should come up on his right. In the center Smith-Dorrien's corps had met and were slowly pushing back German rear guards immensely aided by thick, wooded terrain. On the left Pulteney's corps lacked sufficient materials to bridge the river and still faced considerable opposition, although two battalions found an undefended weir and managed to cross in the afternoon.

On Sir John's right the French were doing little more to aid the hard-pressed Maunoury. Haunted by the same specter of German power that loomed in Sir John French's mind,

Conneau held up his cavalry until a brigade of Maud'huy's infantry came up and pushed into Château-Thierry.

D'Esperey's progress might have been faster but for the increasingly difficult situation of Foch's Ninth Army on his right. With one corps already loaned to Foch, the Fifth Army commander throughout the afternoon increasingly oriented his two center corps toward the northeast or away from advance in line with the BEF.

Perhaps he decided well. From left to right the Ninth Army was yielding its positions to the determined German thrusts. On the height of Mondement, which offered access to the critical ridge of Allemant, seemingly nothing could dislodge a German force increased now to two battalions defending the old château. While French artillery rained on and around the German penetration and prevented enemy guns from coming up, Dubois ordered his reserve to assault the position in early afternoon. The first attempt saw one battalion decimated by deadly fire pouring from every corner of the thick stone walls and buildings of the estate. The attackers, their battalion commander dead, now backed off, sent for heavy guns.[9]

By this time the equally critical height, Mont Août, was in German hands with the 77s firing mercilessly on the open plains to the south. While Foch exhorted his commanders to undertake impossible counterattacks and while Weygand, his chief of staff, personally tried to reorganize the shattered right, Grossetti's 42d Division, having extricated itself from the left with tremendous difficulty, was marching with maddening slowness to the beleaguered right.

The same violent action continued to the east where Langle's right was fighting hard to hold its ground. Similarly, Sarrail's right continued to give way before the weight of the rest of the German Fifth Army.

This was the general situation about 1400 on September 9, 1914.

But now Quast, commanding the German attack against

Maunoury, received orders from First Army Headquarters to break off the action and join a general retreat.

Completely bewildered, Quast called Kuhl, who confirmed the order. Still not satisfied, the aggressive commander sent an aide to argue with Kluck. Despite Quast's urging, Kluck refused to consider any other course of action. With that Quast sent down orders for his front-line units to disengage and fall back.

During the afternoon and evening of September 9, Helmuth von Moltke began to reap the reports of his subordinate's journey. From Bülow he learned,

The First Army is retreating . . . the Second Army, in agreement with Hentsch, is suspending its attack which was progressing slowly, and is retiring to the north bank of the Marne, right wing Dormans. Reinforcements extremely urgent and necessary.[10]

Hentsch called OHL next, reported the retreat of the First Army, then Hausen signaled that he was going to retire the Third Army north of the Marne.

But the German Emperor Wilhelm, supported by various of Moltke's staff officers, had made it quite clear that the center and left offensives must not be abandoned. Accordingly, that night Moltke ordered,

The Third Army will remain south of Châlons, ready for a new offensive; the Fifth Army will attack during the night of the 9th to the 10th; the Fourth Army will also attack, if it has prospects of success. To this end, establish liaison with the Third Army.[11]

Hausen, quite ill from dysentery, confused and now despairing, could see his right flank turned if he followed the new orders from OHL. Telephoning Fourth Army Headquarters, he got hold of Hentsch who was stopping there for the night, and explained the situation to him. Hentsch, apparently more sure of himself than ever and convinced that OHL was hopelessly out of touch with reality, authorized Hausen to retire as he desired.

Hausen was still debating his next move when a peremptory order reached him from OHL: he was to remain south
of the Marne and resume the offensive as soon as possible.
Reverting now to his earlier plan he ordered his right wing
to fall back in contact with Bülow's left, his own left to
maintain its positions and prepare to continue the attack the
next day.

Evening closed on the battle line.

Somewhere along that immense strip of carnage lay a
corpse identified by his tags as Marie-Lucien Guillard. He was
not long dead and in searching him for life someone found a
letter in his bloodied tunic and mailed it. This was what a
young soldier wrote on September 9, 1914, shortly before he
died:

My good and dear ones,—
  When this letter reaches you, your child will have gone to
heaven, unless some kind Germans may have rescued him on the
field of battle. Yesterday morning, September 8, at about half-past
six, while you were at mass, owing to the holy will of Providence,
I was struck by a ball which went through my thigh and I fell. I
am still in the same spot, for, by a truly unworthy similarity with
the fate of my Saviour Jesus on the Cross, I am actually nailed to
my Cross, being unable to move my leg even the smallest part
of an inch. My wound is not very painful, provided I do not stir,
but I am suffering desperately from thirst. My morale is excellent,
I am enduring no agony. My crucifix is before my eyes. I pray
and I await the will of my good God. You knew that, before I
left, I had made a vow to sacrifice my life. I have renewed this
vow many times since yesterday morning. I renew it again now
with all that may be pleasing to God to add or to retract. I have
no fear of death; I have seen it and I see it still too near me even
as I write. There is nothing horrible about it, because it brings
happiness. As for yourselves, I pray that your grief will be silent,
resigned, almost joyful. My greatest sorrow is to leave you, but I
know that before long I shall find you again.[12]

North of the Ourcq exhausted French soldiers had been wondering for several hours at the lessening of the German pressure. No matter the reason, it was a respite grandly welcomed, and as local commanders ordered hasty emplacements dug and lines straightened and positions restored, generals in the rear wondered how they were to hold against the attacks certain to begin again on the morrow.

In the south the BEF failed to recover from its earlier checks. On Sir John's right Haig's corps remained halted until about 1500, when aviators reported "all clear" on the front ahead. Then preceded by cavalry the infantry columns resumed the march and soon reached the vital Château-Thierry–Montreuil road.

Here they again halted, this time on Sir John's orders. With two of his corps engaged, with no French cavalry on his right, he had no intention of advancing against what he thought was the best part of two enemy corps. Had he thought to use his aircraft in their proper role he soon would have learned what slight forces covered his army front. Instead, most of the machines were "employed to discover the positions of the heads of the British columns and what was happening on the British right and left," tasks "which should have been done by motorcycle despatch riders from the divisions, and by liaison officers with the French armies on our flanks."[13]

Even without air Haig's continued advance would soon have disclosed the truth. If the BEF instead of advancing less than twelve miles on September 9 had pushed fifteen or twenty miles forward, they would have netted a tactical victory that possibly could have become decisive. Instead, by the time one of Conneau's cavalry divisions came up on Haig's right and further reports from Henderson's aviators confirmed a retreat of the German armies, the striking hour had passed. No more was Maud'huy able to bring his corps into play against the highly vulnerable German columns on his front. Together with Conneau's cavalry French infantry spent the night at Château-Thierry.

Meanwhile the frantic situation faced by Foch continued throughout the afternoon. Although an artillery shield prevented the enemy from reinforcing his penetration in the Château de Mondement, not until late evening did heavy guns arrive to open nearly point-blank fire against the heavy walls. This time an infantry assault gained the enclosure only to see the backs of a few defenders scrambling down the rugged slopes toward the St. Gond marshes—the German commander had received orders earlier to retreat, but despite his own wounds had remained until his wounded were evacuated.[14]

Simultaneously Weygand's efforts to organize a counterattack on the right proved futile, the more so since Grossetti's division never did arrive. In less than two days the French had fired nearly 100,000 rounds of 75-mm. high explosive and shrapnel at the persistent enemy, but since late afternoon the vigor of his advance had lessened, and when at last Weygand succeeded in moving forward an infantry brigade it discovered that the enemy was gone.

No one on the French side quite realized what had happened. D'Esperey came closest in a proclamation that night to the Fifth Army: "Held on his flanks, his center broken, the enemy is now retreating toward the east and north by forced marches."

But on the right Foch could scarcely believe that the enemy's center was broken; on the left, Sir John French, Maunoury and Galliéni were scarcely convinced that the enemy's right flank was held.

No more did Joffre and his officers at GQG sense the exact situation. Although pleased at the day's action, as Joffre saw it,

. . . the enemy seems to have retreated, partly in the forests north of Champaubert, and on the Marne above Château-Thierry, partly on the line Etrépilly–Courchamps, where he seems to be entrenching. These forces are extended to the left by those facing the Sixth Army.[15]

On the German side, Kluck knew what was going on, of course, so did Kuhl, Bülow, Lauenstein, Hausen and Hentsch. At Luxembourg Moltke still held only a cloudy picture of the actual positions of his armies.

But more than Joffre and more than any of the German staff officers and generals, Helmuth von Moltke knew what had happened and in a letter that night to his wife presciently forecast its meaning:

Things are going badly, the battles east of Paris will not be decided in our favor.... The war which began with such good hopes will in the end go against us.... We shall be crushed in the fight against East and West.... Our campaign is a cruel disillusion. And we shall have to pay for all the destruction which we have done.[16]

Moltke was quite correct. Although neither side had named the long battle and although spasmodic fighting would continue along the line, when dawn broke on September 10 the Battle of the Marne had ended—and so had German hopes for "a swift, crushing victory" in the west.

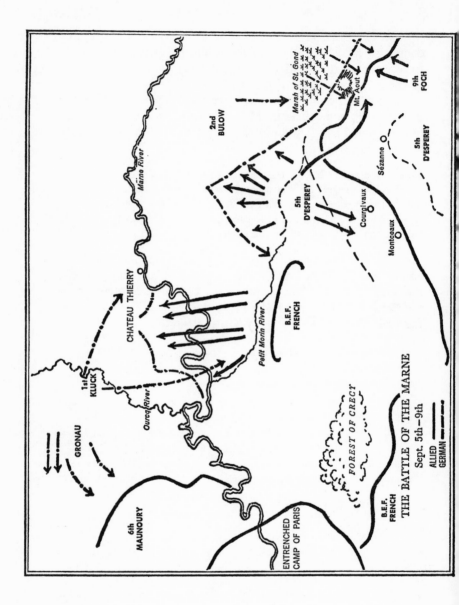

THE BATTLE OF THE MARNE
Sept. 5th–9th

ALLIED

GERMAN

# "VICTORY IS NOW IN THE
# LEGS OF THE INFANTRY . . . "

13  THE BATTLE OF THE MARNE was over, the German
retreat had begun. Black as the situation was for the Germans,
on the morning of September 10 Hentsch learned more bad
news at Fifth Army Headquarters. Sarrail's artillery, firing on
pre-registered targets, had taken the wind out of the Crown
Prince's pre-dawn attack and a conventional frontal attack
had bogged down.

Conflict now developed. According to Prince Wilhelm,
Hentsch briefed him on the general situation and ordered the
Fifth Army to retreat but refused to put the order in writing.
According to Hentsch, he agreed with the royal commander
that the Fifth Army should stand on its positions. In either
event, tempers seem to have boiled over before Hentsch
departed to report to Moltke at Luxembourg.

Moltke's own temper was not improved on the same
morning when Kluck's rather pointed message of the previous
evening arrived:

The right wing of the First Army was driving back the enemy
in the direction of Nanteuil; the center and left wing were main-
taining their positions. The II Cavalry Corps was holding the
enemy in check on the Marne at La Ferté and above. The First

Army retired in conformity to an order of the High Command, not pressed by the French. . . . The British are progressing beyond the Marne. . . . Intention for the 10th: to continue the movement north of the Aisne. . . .[1]

Moltke next received Bülow's more politic message:

In agreement with Hentsch, I judge the situation as follows: the retreat of the First Army behind the Aisne was required by the strategical and tactical situation. The Second Army must support the First north of the Marne. . . . Will reach today Dormans–Avize, with a strong rear guard south of the Marne in liaison with the Third Army. Awaiting orders.[2]

Moltke, of course, had no way of judging the accuracy of these reports nor would he learn the facts until Hentsch arrived later in the day. But he and his staff officers did realize that the retirement routes of the two right-wing armies were not going to close the gap between them. After querying Kluck for further details of his retirement and receiving no reply, Moltke sent him a blunt order: "The First Army will be subordinated until further orders to the commander of the Second Army."

Not sure of a victory to exploit, Joffre issued conservative orders for September 10: the Sixth Army to advance north; the BEF to advance about seven miles northeast; the Fifth Army to advance north, its right supporting the Ninth Army which was to continue its offensive.[3]

From early in the day the Allied advance dragged. What should have developed into a pursuit overwhelming slim enemy rear guards instead remained a cautious series of conservative actions with miles replaced by yards, thousands of prisoners replaced by hundreds.

Fatigue was partly to blame, as was the mistaken notion of enemy forces held by GQG. The weather complicated matters: a night of cold rain left a sky of leaden cloud and heavy mist that grounded aircraft and blinded cavalry patrols.

Of the Allied commanders, Foch pushed his people the hardest despite their shattered condition. Calling on every passion from Motherhood to the Mother Church the little French commander by nightfall had straightened out his decimated units, pushed his right to the north.

By late afternoon advance guards of d'Esperey's right moved across the Marne, but on his left in the vital area Maud'huy moved only cautiously toward the river while his cavalry, practically on tiptoes, finally managed to cross and push patrols five miles to the north.[4]

Sir John French had not received Joffre's newest orders when the BEF moved out at 0500. On the right British cavalry soon ran into heavy artillery fire, spent the morning fighting a series of small actions hindered by muddy ground that slowed the advance of horse artillery. Similarly, Haig struck fortified positions on his right, his subsequent deployment and attack being disrupted by a British battery mistakenly shelling its own infantry.[5] Smith-Dorrien pushed forward slowly in the center, fighting a series of successful but time-consuming actions and capturing numerous prisoners and materiel. On the left Pulteney's corps spent the day bridging the Marne. By evening the BEF had advanced only about ten miles.

North of the Marne Maunoury's patrols early discovered the enemy's withdrawal, but not until midafternoon could his weary, shattered and disorganized divisions respond to his orders to advance. While Bridoux' cavalry on the left fanned out patrols as far as twenty-five miles without encountering the enemy, the Sixth Army advanced only about nine miles before dark.

Hentsch arrived at Luxembourg in midafternoon, reported the general situation to Moltke and his staff officers, and explained the reasoning behind his actions. Realizing that everything feared at OHL was true, Moltke wasted little time in approving his subordinate's deeds. That evening an official

message directed the four right-wing armies to retire to designated lines while the Fifth Army stood its present positions.
And now, when defeat could only be compounded,
Moltke decided to visit the front. Early on September 11 he
left Luxembourg by motorcar. Enormously depressed, he
fervently grasped at the straws of defeat everywhere seen:
the French holding the heights of the Meuse, the little
fort of Troyon still defying capture, the Fifth Army's frontal
offensive stopped, the Third Army spread weakly with no
reserves, then a report of a new advance in strength toward
the Third Army's right. Almost as if he had been waiting for
the opportunity the Chief of the Great General Staff now
acted finally and irrevocably.

On the afternoon of September 11, Helmuth von Moltke
in the name of his Emperor ordered the retirement of the
Third, Fourth and Fifth Armies behind the Vesle and Aisne
Rivers.

By the night of September 10 Joffre knew the battle was
won. Now he ordered the Sixth Army and the BEF to push
north on either side of the Ourcq; the Fifth Army to strike
east against the columns retreating before Foch's Ninth
Army; Foch to advance east in conjunction with the Fourth
Army attacking north; the Third Army to hold its positions.[6]
Further, "to confirm and exploit this success, the advance
must be pursued energetically, leaving the enemy no respite;
victory is now in the legs of the infantry."

The legs of the infantry were either too tired or too
confused to conform, nor did low weather followed by high
winds and a cold drenching rain help.

Although fighting only minor skirmishes, Maunoury's
Sixth Army advanced but nine miles during September 11.
The BEF encountered virtually no enemy but with its divisions
confined to single roads and with Pulteney's corps held up by a
French column progress again was slow, about ten miles
being covered. Joffre's orders to d'Esperey spelled delay in

the Fifth Army; Foch's Ninth Army managed to advance ten to fifteen miles, Langle rather less.

Still, no one could doubt the victory nor the hard fighting that had made it so. Carrion birds hovered over the fields: thousands of bodies covered the Barcy plateau, the plains of Fère Champenoise, the fields of Vitry, the hills of the Grand Couronné. German equipment and personal kit littered the roads leading to the Aisne. Sarrail's Third Army captured all the artillery of one corps. German wounded by the hundreds were discovered in hastily evacuated villages and cities such as Châlons where the enemy left a thousand casualties despite an earlier, unjust demand for 30 million francs in reparations.[7]

Joffre formally announced the Allied victory on September 11, but GQG held no illusions about the extent of it. The next day, his chief of operations told the American military attaché, "The retreat, of course, is not a rout, but is being conducted by Germany in good order. . . ."[8]

Despite Joffre's best efforts the pursuit was not going to pick up. By September 12 Germany's right wing was trickling into prepared defenses behind the Aisne, the BEF and the French breathing hot on the German rear guards. But now a corps from Alsace and one from Maubeuge positioned between Kluck's and Bülow's armies to close the fatal gap and present a solid line to the Allies.

At 0115, September 15, Joffre telegraphed his commanders:

It seems as if the enemy is once more going to accept battle in prepared positions north of the Aisne. In consequence it is no longer a question of pursuit but of methodical attack.[9]

These were momentous words, for they rang down the curtain on a stage of hopes. Act I of the great war drama— the campaign of the Marne—was played out. Gone now on either side were any pretensions to swift, crushing victory. Gone now on either side were any illusions of the glory and romance of modern warfare.

The French won the campaign, but there was little to

applaud in the victory. Wounded filled the hospitals, dead covered the fields, tons of materiel and guns had been lost, the enemy had retired still able to fight.

Now there would be a pause between acts, a shifting of human scenery along the stage from the Alps to the' English Channel. Then the curtain would rise again.

In Act II there would be no more mobile warfare. This time the play would take place in trenches. This time the act would last for four years.

# SUMMING UP: I

14   THE HUMAN COST of the campaign and its climax, the battle, was very high. The few official records that do exist cannot be verified—excepting the British, the figures are probably too low, for citizens were not yet inured to slaughter and governments were afraid to tell the truth.

Many years after the war France put her total casualties for August and September at 329,000 (out of a total of 1,796,000 for the entire war). Subtracting 20 per cent for the later September battles on the Meuse, in the Argonne, at St. Mihiel and the march to the sea, this leaves an approximate total of a quarter-million French casualties.[1]

The BEF from the beginning of the campaign to September 10, 1914, recorded 12,733 total casualties, 1701 of them suffered from September 6–10.[2]

The German official history did not include casualty figures, but unit records, eye-witness accounts and telling phrases from various command reports offer some idea of their extent. Unit after unit reported themselves at half-strength with 20 and 30 per cent, sometimes higher, officer casualties. The Battle of the Frontiers hurt all armies, Le Cateau and Guise–St. Quentin the two right-wing armies. Kluck's losses were high at the battle of the Ourcq—as has been said, the plateau of Barcy resembled a huge above-ground cemetery, the trenches at Vareddes and Etrépilly were jammed with dead, the hospitals and churches were full of abandoned German wounded. Bülow on September 7 reported that "because of heavy losses" he had only "the strength of three army corps," and Hentsch, in his later formal report to OHL, wrote that the Second Army was "burnt out to a cinder." On September 12 "tremendous amounts of dead and wounded" still remained around Fère Champenoise and Vitry-le-François; French officers there estimated 30,000 killed and 120,000 wounded, each side taking about half.[3] Both Hausen and Crown Prince Wilhelm planned surprise pre-dawn attacks because of the havoc created in their daylight formations by the French 75s. In Lorraine, official Bavarian figures put *Bavarian losses alone*[4] up to September 14 at 17,000 killed and 49,000 wounded out of a total 300,000. The 3rd Bavarian Division itself lost 7700. Finally, during the German retreat to the Aisne the Allies captured over 15,000 prisoners.

When Falkenhayn took command of the German Army on September 14 he found its "fighting strength greatly reduced; everywhere a shortage of junior officers, huge gaps in the ranks."[5] Yet he found an army quite able to fight and for this reason numerous writers have stated that the Battle of the Marne was not a tactical victory for the Allies, indeed that something supernatural lay behind the German retreat—the so-called "miracle of the Marne."[6]

Obviously the French and British did not win a decisive victory, nor even a great one such as that of the Germans when they captured an entire Russian army at Tannenberg, or that of the Russians when they captured 100,000 Austrians at Lemberg. But a tactical victory, or superiority of tactics in a given military situation, is nonetheless a victory, and in this case an impressive one for the Allies.

Fundamental to French tactics at the beginning of the war was the concept of the *offensive à outrance*, the all-out offen-

sive which some officers mistakenly translated to bayonet assaults over open ground with no preliminary artillery fire, no
flank protection, no rear-area emplacements. Defeat with heavy
losses forced a defensive withdrawal in which the vicious little
French 75s played the predominant role although the British
stand at Le Cateau and the French action at Guise–St. Quentin
contributed a large part.

Once Joffre resumed the offensive many of the earlier
faults of the *offensive à outrance* were repeated, but now the
spirit of the concept asserted itself and tired, retreating soldiers
suddenly turned and fought and when they were pushed back
they fought like devils to regain what they had lost.

The spirit of the offensive saved France at the Battle of the
Marne, and by saving France it beat Moltke's army. Offensive
tactics forced Kluck to withdraw his left from Bülow's right.
With Maunoury, Foch, Langle and Sarrail holding the other
armies—holding by offensive tactics—the way stood open for
the BEF and d'Esperey's Fifth Army *to advance offensively*.
Had the rupture between Kluck and Bülow been exploited,
again offensively, nothing in the world could have saved the
German line except the additional corps that Schlieffen wanted
and Germany didn't possess.

As it was, had Kluck delayed a day longer at the Ourcq
the BEF would have swarmed over his flank and rear; had
Bülow delayed, d'Esperey's Fifth Army would have rolled up
his right. As for Kluck's traditionally vaunted offensive on
September 9, Quast's group had not yet struck the main line
of French resistance when the withdrawal order reached him,
and Lepel's brigade at Nanteuil had been and was being hit
hard by French artillery. Maunoury had the 8th Division
coming up and, thanks to Kluck's withdrawing his left to the
north, his entire right to draw from. The British were less
than a day's march away, Maunoury's left was backed by Galliéni's second defensive line, another corps was marching to
him from the east. As for Foch's precarious right, nothing was
to prevent him from drawing it back temporarily while d'Es-

perey's Fifth Army struck from the west and the XXI Corps filled the gap on Langle's left.

The "miracle of the Marne" is a shibboleth exactly like the "miracle of Dunkirk."[7] The supernatural has no place on the battlefield. Officers and men win and lose battles. Joffre and Frenchmen and Englishmen won the Battle of the Marne, the Germans lost it. By refusing to be beaten and by somehow transmitting his resolution and determination to his commanders and to his troops, Joffre vindicated for all time the value of the offensive spirit. His was a tactical victory, but it also was a moral and psychological victory.

That Joffre's will did not prevail in the pursuit is explained by the flesh. You cannot have men fight a series of disastrous encounter battles, fall them back a hundred miles, turn them about and fight them again, attack and be attacked, give them spasmodic rations and sleep, then expect them to jump up and move out another fifty miles in time to overtake an enemy still able to resist if he has to.

Without the tactical victory of the actual battle there would have been no strategic victory resulting from the campaign, and this unquestionably was decisive. Shortsighted as were French pre-war plans, abortive as were the opening attacks, the French ability to right matters coupled with German inability to control them spelled nothing less than the end of German hopes as hysterically stated in Moltke's letter to his wife.

War on two fronts! Exactly what every General Staff planner from Moltke the Elder to Schlieffen had feared. With the end of mobile warfare went any chance of swift "decisive" victory, even of favorably negotiated peace. By forcing the Germany Army into trench warfare the Allies brought upon her country the specter of attrition, and this she was not prepared to meet.

Primary responsibility for Germany's defeat at the Marne must go to Moltke and his influence on the Schlieffen strategy.

When Moltke accepted Germany's supreme military post in 1906 he embarked on the job with a traditional freedom of action emphasized in his case by being the Emperor's favorite. Moltke need not have accepted Schlieffen's operational legacy any more than Schlieffen had accepted that bequeathed to him by the elder Moltke and Waldersee.

The root of Moltke's full-blown failure stemmed from his accepting a strategy, a very daring one, without having the courage to accept the tactical gamble necessary to carry it out. Any offensive plan against numerically superior forces is risky, but one talent demanded by the military art is the reduction of planning uncertainties to hard facts—pleasant or sad. If investigation leaves too many uncertainties or turns up too many unpleasant facts, then the plan must be sacrificed in favor of another.

Instead of testing the tactical demands of the Schlieffen strategy, then making his decision, Moltke accepted it, then proceeded to modify it in an attempt to gain what doesn't exist: a "safe" gamble. By 1914 the tactical portion of the plan bore little resemblance to that envisioned by Schlieffen. As modified by Moltke it contained all the disadvantages of the earlier plan, few of the advantages.

Were there advantages in the basic plan? The most recent writing on the subject—Gerhard Ritter's *The Schlieffen Plan* —points out Schlieffen's own doubts about his 1905 Memorandum, and concludes that the whole excursion was so risky as to be invalid. No one, of course, can prove whether Schlieffen was right or wrong—certainly his disregard of Belgian and Dutch neutrality was bound to earn Germany the censure of the world, while Dutch military resistance would have offered him another, albeit slight problem which he thought to handle with two divisions.

But Ritter's seeming implication that Schlieffen was the real villain seems unjust since he did not bear operational or command responsibility; nor do Ritter's attempts to denigrate Schlieffen's strategy seem wholly justified by fact.

Moltke's two major modifications before the war lay in

changing the ratio of strength from right to left from 8:1 to 3:1, and in scrapping the plan to invade Holland. When the war started he used his *Ersatz* divisions to reinforce his left, not his right, which meant that Kluck shed a corps to shield Antwerp and a brigade to garrison Brussels. When the time came to transfer troops to the eastern front, instead of taking six corps equitably, one from each of the armies, Moltke took two from a right wing that already had sacrificed impressive strength to perform low-priority garrison and siege tasks.

Moltke's *coup de main* against Liége bogged down because by not attacking through Holland he forfeited the tremendous advantage of immediate assault against the Liége forts from the north. In return he gained but little: his invasion of Belgium proved an immediate moral defeat which a simultaneous invasion of Holland could scarcely have compounded. His hope to keep Holland as a neutral "windpipe" seems rather ridiculous in view of the British fleet; he probably did save himself another military action, but it seems reasonable that one corps could have screened his right flank against the Dutch Army if Holland had chosen to fight. As a result of his reasoning, Kluck's First Army, ready to march from Aix-la-Chapelle on August 10, marched a week later, a delay reflected in the the other right-wing armies.

Assuming the Belgian Army would have withdrawn to Antwerp had Kluck marched earlier—it would have been annihilated otherwise—Kluck and Bülow on his left would have crossed the border into France before the BEF ever reached Mons, thus realizing Kitchener's worst fears of the BEF's being caught while detraining.

Even the way it happened the story would have been altered by Kluck's retaining an additional corps. When on August 20 he was marching west towards Lille–Tournai and was ordered south by Bülow to guard the Second Army's flank at the Sambre, he argued strongly for continuing on his original course. Forced to conform, since he was temporarily under Bülow's orders, he ran head-on into the BEF at Mons.

Strong as were his and Kuhl's feelings, with another corps at their disposal they surely would have extended their right and taken the BEF in a calamitous flank attack with one corps against a hastily improvised British brigade of rear-area personnel. Even with Marwitz' cavalry corps—which Kluck asked for unsuccessfully until August 24—he might have contained the British retreat until bringing his greater strength to bear.

Had the BEF somehow managed to escape this situation, and the French Fifth Army along with it, there seems little doubt that an extra German corps would have changed the outcome of Le Cateau, where Smith-Dorrien by his own admission escaped disaster by the skin of his teeth. Again, on the Ourcq one corps would have made an enormous difference, two corps probably the decisive difference.

Schlieffen, of course, planned many more corps for his right wing, and two objections to his plan may be raised:

(1) The BEF and Lanrezac's Fifth Army would never have put themselves in such vulnerable positions if they had known of an enemy advance;

(2) Roads were not sufficient to support the additional corps nor were railroads sufficient to support them logistically.

The first objection is voided by the surprise of the German advance: utter, complete surprise. As late as August 22 GQG did not imagine that a force in strength was advancing north of the Meuse. Cleverly masked by heavy cavalry forces to throw off any French observers, the German right marched forward, a secret entity of nearly half a million men.

The second objection is much more valid, particularly since Kluck did outrun his supply on several occasions. That ample road space existed through Belgium is proved because up to Antwerp Kluck's army marched in full strength as did Bülow's and Hausen's to Namur. The British official map of 1914 shows five secondary highways running west-southwest out of Mons, numerous minor roads there and in the north.[8] General Poseck points out how German cavalry operations were aided by the well-built network of roads in Belgium and

France.[9] Nearly three British corps fell back from Mons without particular difficulty (there were roads through the Forest of Mormal but British cavalry failed to see them) and on the British left Allenby's cavalry and three French Territorial divisions found ample room for retirement. In a long section in his *Memoirs*, Sir John French described the excellent road network in the Mons area; the official British historian called the highway complex perfectly adequate.[10] These same *routes nationales* led into Paris and became more plentiful in the south —the map clearly shows an excellent lateral roadway system complementing them.

Belgian railways at the time of the German invasion comprised over 2500 miles of standard gauge, another 2500 miles of meter gauge. None of the latter's rolling stock was evacuated into France, some of the standard rolling stock was. Although trains could not pass through Liége until August 24—a handicap that immediate northern attack might have voided—and then only with difficulty, the First Army started operating a light railway system to the forward corps on August 22.[11]

In 1914 the French Nord Railway maintained from two to four double-line major arteries running, for example, from Paris–Soissons–Laon–Hirson or Paris–Amiens–Arras–Lille, with major railheads spotted at such terminals as Charleroi, Mons, Valenciennes and Lille. Numerous single lines ran from Paris to the northeast and an ample lateral system existed along the entire route.[12]

During the retreat to the Marne both the French and British, primarily cavalry, blew rail bridges when and where they could. According to the official British transport historian, "the total amount of damage done was comparatively slight, most of the breaks being made hurriedly by field troops with a limited stock of explosives."[13] Moltke's transport chief, Lieutenant Colonel Gröner, controlled no less than 90 companies of railway repair troops who stood ready with equipment that included portable, sectionalized railway bridges up to 200 feet long.[14]

That the right-wing armies seemed unconcerned with supply by rail must surely be accountable to design, not choice. No effort, for example, was made to storm Maubeuge, a vital railway terminal, yet a fortress-city in so ghastly a state of defense that it scarcely warranted the two weeks it took to capture. Schlieffen's strategy called for a victory against France in six weeks—not a prolonged campaign depending on rail support.

Admittedly German shortages in artillery shells developed, a false estimate of field requirements also shared by the French who immediately after the Marne faced a real shortage and took extreme measures to meet it.[15] Units did outrun supply trains and in some cases field kitchens which, incidentally, were a remarkable innovation at the time and attest to careful pre-war planning for field mobility.

But the invasion route scarcely passed through a wasteland. Kluck noted that on August 23 Marwitz' cavalry watered their horses in the Schelde where oats laid in stooks in abundance.[16] Again, the IV Reserve Corps in its march through Amiens captured an enormous quantity of supply, and in Noyon a vast amount of oats, straw and hay was found. Kluck noted further that the season of the year favored the campaign, especially as regarded the provision of an abundant and, for the most part, wholesome supply of food.[17]

Kluck admitted that the supply services ran into difficulties as early as August 20 and that after August 30, "the further course of the campaign was to make the greatest possible demands on the capacity of the transport and supply columns, the life-blood of the Army."[18]

From Alexander the Great to General George Patton there has never been a swift-moving commander who hasn't outrun his supply, hasn't faced immense logistic difficulties and sometimes the problem of hungry troops. That does not mean the fighting capability is eliminated. Captain Bloem noted as early as before Mons,

---

We had out-marched our communications. Not once had the supply columns got up to us, and we had had to live on the country, fortunately a very well-stocked one, taking what we could find. Of coffee, meat, potatoes and vegetables there was no lack—only bread that failed us completely, and I now learnt for the first time what a vitally important part bread plays in the life of the working man.[19]

Going into the Battle of the Marne,

In Taillefontaine village, not far from Paris, they [his men] found seventy-five loaves of white bread in the cellar of a baker's shop . . . at Largny, not far from Paris, we halted on a bare hillside and the cookers came forward.

On September 4,

The supply columns from the rear seldom reached us, and we still lived on the country, so that the daily rations were often sketchy. The company butchers, Eberling and Liebsch, working day and night in the most difficult circumstances . . . were able to maintain a sufficient supply of meat.

During the Battle of the Marne his cookers came up frequently and his troops also ate in many of the village houses.[20]

That Kluck's troops and the rest of the German right were tired, often hungry, is true; that this seems any more nearly to have vitiated their combat capability than it did the French, for example Humbert's Moroccans at Mondement, is denied both by personal accounts of soldiers on the scene and by the very rugged fighting that continued through September 9 and even during the German retreat. Using the experience of the units at the Marne as a guide-rule, there is no reason that the countryside to the richer west could not have supported one, two or three more German corps who like their brethren would have marched, not ridden in trains. Moreover had Moltke and the General Staff properly studied the logistic requirement before the war, as did the British, it seems probable that skillful railway experts could have utilized the adequate French railway system from the Belgian border to Paris.

In truth Moltke was never sold on the essential Schlieffen strategy, which was too bold for his nature. Unwilling to yield German territory on his left any more than Joffre and his staff officers were willing to yield French territory, under pressure by the royal commanders of the left and center armies, undoubtedly influenced by powerful critics of Schlieffen including Bülow, holding the British threat in utter contempt as did all German commanders, Moltke nearly had made up his mind to fight an offensive in Lorraine when the war began.

His wavering attitude was not aided by Intelligence or communication failures nor by false reports submitted by his army commanders. One can disdain but not ignore an army in the strength of 100,000; yet on August 20, three days before Kluck ran into the BEF, OHL did not even know the English had arrived in France, much less were waiting on the Condé canal. (No more at a later date, when it was too late to matter, could OHL accurately assess the rumor of large British troop landings at Ostend.) In fact, sitting back in Coblenz Moltke held only the dimmest idea of the forward action, a sort of interested oblivion that continued when he moved to Luxembourg.

German front-to-rear communications were hopeless. Radio was in its infancy, telephones were scarcely reliable, cable-wireless was slow and uncertain. OHL operated only one radio receiver—as incredible as this may seem. Although Moltke remained out of touch with his right wing for long periods and at times of extreme crisis,

practically nothing was done to extend without delay the inadequate communications between Luxembourg and the right wing of the armies, or to improve them by making use of the various supplementary technical means of communication: wireless, cable, motors, airplanes.[21]

Failure of army commanders to report fully rests partly on technical deficiencies, partly on their own obstinacy and ambition. When Hausen split the Third Army, giving a group to Albrecht and one to Bülow, he failed even to notify Moltke, yet the order stood in contradiction to Moltke's latest Directive. More harmful, though, were the early reports of victory. Whether the local commanders were actually fooled by the French retreats or whether they optimistically sensed crushing victories if allowed to continue their offensives, they sent a stream of reports so false to OHL that any one message would have been legitimate grounds for court-martial. Not once, with the exception of Hentsch, did Moltke send liaison officers to see for themselves what was going on—he felt that this would have implied distrust of the commanders.[22]

Weak to the point of effeteness, Moltke's conduct during the first weeks of the war resembled that of an impotent orchestral conductor whose players, frequently disregarding the baton, turn a splendidly composed military march into a cacophony of discord so great as to send the conductor whimpering from the podium, a shattered man wallowing to his death in the weakness of an entire life.

Moltke already had given up during the Battle of the Marne—the rest was mere formality. On September 14 the Emperor relieved him in favor of Falkenhayn. Having announced to the world that the Battle of the Marne was in reality a German victory, OHL could not now announce that the Chief of the Great General Staff had been sacked: until early November the fact remained a secret. Then the announcement was made, Moltke left OHL, a sick old man who died in 1916 —impossible to defend but not to pity.

After Moltke's death Hentsch fell heir to the blame for German defeat at the Marne. Quiet at first, the criticism grew with every subsequent defeat. Finally, in 1917 and shortly before Hentsch's death in Rumania, Hindenburg as Chief of the Great General Staff ordered a formal board of inquiry to investigate the case. In Ludendorff's Memorandum embodying the results,

. . . Colonel Hentsch incurs no personal reproach that he went beyond what he was entitled to do. He acted solely in accordance with the instructions given to him by the then Chief of the German General Staff of the Field Army.[23]

Despite these findings the Hentsch controversy continued —and still does.

# SUMMING UP: II

15 THE AUTHOR of Plan XVII, Joffre, has been blamed for the abortive opening battles of the war; in his effort to adjust this strategy, which included relieving a good many generals, he has been condemned for trying to shift the blame; in his subsequent direction of battle he has been accused of strategic blunders ranging from his overlooking the opportunity for counterattack presented by Kluck's advance across the Marne, an error allegedly repaired by Galliéni, to his willingness to sacrifice the fortress of Verdun, an error supposedly repaired by Sarrail.

A large portion of Joffre's troubles stemmed from the muddled situation of the French Army when he assumed the top post in 1911. Forty years of defeatist thinking could not be removed overnight, no matter the martial ardor aroused by Grandmaison's clarion call to action, yet it fell to Joffre to attempt to do exactly this—to reorganize a vast army torn with dissension, its ranks filled with incompetence as its depots were filled with obsolescence—to train it for the war everyone knew was coming, and to fight it in such a way that France would win.

That this had to be some form of offensive action was

taken for granted. Joffre was very much an officer of his day; had he not subscribed to the general principles of the *offensive à outrance*, he never would have been given the supreme job. He was no more willing than the other members of this school to yield French territory to an enemy, a blind spot explained by the emotional fervor inherent in the Army's aggressive renascence. This was a mistake, but failure made it so.

The next question was how best to employ the offensive. Michel's imaginative plan contained two fallacies, or so the General Staff believed. To shift the center of weight from right to left necessitated a change of attitude on Belgium's part or a French decision to violate Belgian neutrality upon the outbreak of war. Belgium made it quite clear that she was playing an independent game; England made it just as clear that if France invaded Belgium she would fight Germany without English help.

Just possibly Belgium's intransigence might have been overcome by skillful diplomacy, but now faulty Intelligence entered the play. Joffre's major advisers, primarily Castelnau, held that Germany did not have enough troops to extend her right in a wide sweep through Belgium, a conventional belief at a time when no country employed reserve troops alongside regular formations and when experienced officers such as General Pau frankly distrusted the fighting ability of reserves. Unfortunately Joffre and his other advisers believed this and so remained blind to certain pre-war indications of German intentions and to the actual course of events in the first weeks of war.

As Chief of the General Staff Joffre of course must bear overall responsibility for these errors. That he admits them and does accept blame makes his *Memoirs* the more refreshing, particularly when compared with the self-righteous, highly critical outpourings of other principals. That his advisers from Galliéni to Foch equally erred should be remembered, as should Belgium's pre-war attitude, particularly in view of her whimperings about being let down by the Allies.

Once the ugly truth of the German plan was established, along with the obvious failure of Plan XVII, Joffre had to act and act in a hurry. The great retreat to the Marne succeeded for several reasons: Smith-Dorrien's stand at Mons and his unpremeditated and very courageous stand at Le Cateau surprised, hurt and slowed Kluck besides confusing him. Lanrezac's stand at Guise–St. Quentin accomplished the same with Bülow. The more or less equality in numbers gave the advantage to the defender, particularly where he could bring into action the superior 75-mm. gun. Finally, and by far the most important, the maneuver was conducted by a man who refused to become hysterical, refused to believe he was beaten, insisted that his will be imposed throughout his army.

To Joffre in those very dark days of what seemed nearly complete defeat the question no longer was the failure of Plan XVII or who was responsible or why. Instead it was the very real question of survival, of extreme sacrifice until his army was safe and could again return to the offensive. It was not a time for normal amenities, for long personal debates before removing this officer or that. Joffre was asking the maximum of his subordinates; if he could not trust one of them to offer it or if the maximum effort of one of them did not suit him then that general had to go.

Some he suffered longer than others, probably from loyalty. Lanrezac was one. Probably no other officer in the French Army stood higher in Joffre's estimation than this moody colonial. Before the war he had proved a model general, a brilliant tactician and thinker whose lectures became famous throughout the officer corps. Yet with war began a disintegration the more tragic because it stemmed from Lanrezac's half-correct estimate of German intentions.

No more than Joffre or Berthelot or Belin or any of the others except Michel did Lanrezac assess the true breadth of the German maneuver,[1] yet Joffre's failure to heed the half-warning caused his subordinate to begin an insubordinate sulk that never ceased. Lanrezac's false report on August 23 of the

BEF's position, his willingness to sacrifice the BEF to the enemy,[2] his behavior at Guise–St. Quentin—each was sufficient reason for any commander to relieve him on the spot, but even then Joffre held off.

Only when he realized that Lanrezac's continued presence would jeopardize the BEF's participation in the new offensive did he act. He had to. Without the BEF he could not hope to win.

Nowhere is Joffre's patience more remarkably exhibited than in his relations with Sir John French. French was extremely difficult. In aloofness and caution he resembled the German Moltke, but he also owned a basic courage akin to Joffre's that more than once allowed him to face up to unpleasant reality and act in what he deemed to be the best interest of all concerned. That this was generally in his own interest reflects no more than a human failing. French was human and he also was English, which explains why his main difficulty was not that he acted on a code of a very personal nature, but that he expected other men of other nations to act on it as well.

The only time during the campaign that anyone saw the French commander-in-chief unduly depressed occurred when Henry Wilson met him returning from still another futile conference with Sir John. Seemingly nothing could make the British commander stand to fight—except Kitchener. When French refused every argument mustered by Joffre, not once but time and again, this was the last step to be taken and Joffre took it and it worked. Joffre himself found Sir Archibald Murray the arch-villain. "It was a great relief to us when . . . General Murray was called back to England."[3]

If Joffre erred in his initial selection of commanders and if he were ruthless in cleaning out those found wanting, he nonetheless recognized the abilities of many, promotions for which he would not have to apologize. Pétain, Foch, Maud'huy, d'Esperey, Mangin, Weygand, Gamelin, Nivelle—

Joffre promoted each and each wrote a brilliant chapter across the pages of the war.

Considering that there had been no major war since 1871 it perhaps is not strange that so many persons found Joffre's methods repugnant. What in fact he was doing from the first day of war was commanding. Not only would he brook no nonsense from subordinates, he would tolerate no interference from superiors. When Minister of War Messimy on August 5 sent Galliéni to GQG to forward Messimy's ideas of strategy, Joffre abruptly walked out in the middle of the conference. When Messimy authorized him to have shot any officer not doing his duty, Joffre ignored the offer as impractical. When later Clemenceau pressured him not to relieve Sarrail, Joffre also ignored him—at the ultimate cost of his own career. Aside from Berthelot, Belin and on one occasion Henry Wilson, he refused to discuss strategy with anyone; when Berthelot or staff officers disagreed with him he always listened, sometimes changed his mind.

That is why it is somehow futile to spend much time on the Joffre-Galliéni-Paris controversy. The popular story has it that by September 4 Joffre had decided to retire his armies behind the Seine, when the Governor of Paris, General Galliéni, excitedly telephoned GQG to announce Kluck's change of course and demand permission to attack with Maunoury's Sixth Army. The implied picture of Joffre is of a myopic old fool huddled in GQG, blind to anything but imminent defeat. The tellers, and they were many, forgot that the so-called Galliéni plan of September 4 had been anticipated by Joffre in his General Instructions Number Two of August 25, a plan frustrated but not once forgotten during subsequent events.

Joffre, of course, was perfectly aware of the significance of Kluck's continued advance. Unlike Galliéni he also was aware that an isolated counterattack would accomplish nothing unless it failed, then it would lose France the war. Unlike Galliéni he knew from bitter experience that Sir John French would not support the attack (this was before Kitchener's visit had made itself felt) and he knew, too, that his Fifth and Fourth Armies stood in very shaky condition. He had to investigate each of these $x$ factors before he could act, he did exactly this, and he decided to fight. Far from forcing him to a decision, Galliéni's influence was less than d'Esperey's, for where Galliéni's conference with the British chief of staff, Archibald Murray, produced only equivocation and continuance of the BEF retreat, d'Esperey's meeting with Henry Wilson offered a solid if overoptimistic plan of action, the plan Joffre finally decided to use. Though fully crediting d'Esperey, Joffre did not for a second relinquish the reins of command. If he had not wanted the Battle of the Marne it most certainly would not have been fought.

Joffre was too much the soldier to have it otherwise. Long after the event he remarked, "I do not know who won the Battle of the Marne, but if it had been lost, I know who would have lost it."[4] Although he handled his commanders as the individuals they were, showing patience here, tact there, anger on occasion, he never hesitated to intervene when he sensed that the overall decision was at stake.

Joffre was not a great commander but events made him so. Yet events and all the emotion and passion called forth by them did not change his fundamental character and this is the secret of his greatness at the Marne. It was Joffre's will, not that Kluck should be temporarily checked, or Paris temporarily saved, but that the entire German invasion should be smashed. This was his will, and by imposing it first on his own temporarily beaten armies, next on the temporarily victorious enemy, this was his greatness. It could be said of Joffre as Bosquet long before said of Turenne that he could fight without anger, win without ambition and triumph without vanity. That is a fitting epitaph for Joffre.

# THE MARNE, THE
# WAR AND HISTORY

16 NONE OF THE GENERALS, Allied or enemy, quite realized what had happened in those brief weeks of war. Certain tactical secrets, of course, were now exposed, certain tactical changes were resulting from technological innovations. German mobile heavy artillery had scored major successes, but so had the French 75-mm. gun. The machine gun showed itself particularly devastating in the defense, but so did the modern rifle when fired by a British soldier. Motorcycles and automobiles were proving themselves, so were airplanes, but each side had them and would continue to employ them.

After the war Sir John French wrote in his memoirs,

I cannot help wondering why none of us realized what the most modern rifle, the machine gun, motor traction, the airplane and wireless telegraphy would bring about. . . . I feel sure in my own mind that had we realized the true effect of modern appliances of war in August, 1914, there would have been no retreat from Mons, and that if, in September, the Germans had learnt their lesson, the Allies would never have driven them back to the Aisne.

By the end of the Marne campaign, neither side had yet fully realized the effect of modern weapons on the staying power of the defense in lineal warfare. Without vastly superior numbers the sustained offensive was doomed to an "almost but not quite" status that would remain until development of the internal combustion engine offered a new mobility that, enhanced by the third dimension of air power, changed war of lines to war of areas.

Perhaps sensing this in 1914, the enemy made one more try. Scarcely had the German Army fallen back to the entrenched line of the Aisne when Falkenhayn began moving armies north in a last effort to outflank the Allied left. With the Allies matching each German power shift, this brief effort degenerated into "the race to the sea" until the battle line extended from the Alps to the English Channel. The war now moved into trenches—there it remained.

For Germany this was the beginning of the end. The war of mobility which she failed to win at the Marne became the war of stability which she could never hope to win. Since the elder Moltke her military planners had warned at all cost to avoid a two-front war, where attrition would become the dominant factor. Attrition would cost both sides heavily, but where the Allies with their vast fleets and large empires could stand it, Germany could not.

Victory at the Marne had given the Allies the one thing that Germany could not fight: time. With the western war a stalemate, the world now leveled its collective judgment on the actions of Germany and irrevocably shifted its sympathy to the Allied cause. The Allies themselves gained time to raise and equip new armies, bring pressure to bear on Italy to join the cause, even to attempt a new break-through strategy in the Near East to aid Russia.

But with the dismal failure of the brilliantly conceived and shamefully executed Gallipoli operation, Allied eyes soon returned to the western trenches where a war of professionals was rapidly becoming a slaughter of innocents.

Leaders of neither side would admit the stalemate, not even when a single day's offensive cost 60,000 casualties. New weapons were introduced: heavier artillery, poison gas, the tank. All to no avail. Offensive after offensive was stopped by barbed wire and machine guns. Men fell by the hundreds of thousands on both sides.

In the end Germany gave in. From the moment of her defeat at the Marne attrition began gnawing at her vitals. Slowly, at first almost painlessly. She had vast untapped sources of manpower, she called them up, she forced Russia from the war, she won battles in Italy, she nearly broke through on the western front.

Nearly, but never quite. On the western front her new armies were forever being matched by new Allied armies, her costly offensives were met by costly counterattacks, her innovations were met by Allied innovations.

All the while, attrition was doing its job. Finally she grew desperate, finally she introduced unrestricted submarine warfare. This could have but one ultimate result. In 1917 America joined the Allies, lent their side of the scales the necessary weight to win the war.

It was scarcely a victory. The year 1918 saw Germany a defeated nation, the peace made her a beaten nation. The Russian Empire had vanished, so had the Austro-Hungarian Empire. Stability of any sort was gone. Central and Eastern Europe formed a vast power vacuum. Germany lived only on hatred yearning to be avenged.

The countries that could fill the vacuum and keep Germany beaten failed to do so. Victory had sapped the strength of France and England, a human and economic bankruptcy which England alone was to survive with honor. Wilson's attempt to introduce America into world affairs met with a blank refusal at home—America plunged into an isolationism that ended only when Japanese airplanes bombed Pearl Harbor over twenty years later.

Meanwhile there was Germany, also isolated and bankrupt

—but with hatred. When she found Hitler and Hitler found her there was no one to contest the marriage, no one to stamp out the evil spawn of new military might.

As in 1914, so in 1940 Germany again invaded France. This time there was no contest.

# NOTES

# NOTES

CHAPTER 1

1. The historical-political-economic writing covering the period from 1870–1914 is of course enormous, with major areas of disagreement. In this greatly simplified account I have used general works listed in the Bibliography where not otherwise specified.
2. Erich Eyck, *Bismarck and the German Empire*.
3. Walter Görlitz, *The German General Staff*.
4. Viscount Grey, *Twenty-Five Years;* H. H. Asquith, *The Genesis of the War*.
5. Grey, *op. cit.*
6. *Ibid.;* for the Austrian viewpoint, Robert B. Asprey, *The Panther's Feast*.
7. General Erich Ludendorff, *The General Staff and Its Problems*.
8. B. H. Liddell Hart, *A History of the World War 1914-1918*.

9. Emil Ludwig, *July 1914;* James Cameron, *1914*.

CHAPTER 2

1. F. E. Whitton, *Moltke*.
2. General von Cochenhausen, *Von Scharnhorst zu Schlieffen;* Gerhard Ritter, *The Schlieffen Plan*.
3. Waldersee grudgingly accepted a corps command. Although unpopular in the General Staff, he held an excellent military reputation and continued to gain important commands. In 1900 he was named commander-in-chief of the German Expeditionary Force sent to fight the Boxers in China and was promoted to field marshal. He died in 1904. Görlitz, *op. cit.*
4. *Ibid.*
5. Ritter, *op. cit.* This and Schlieffen's other memoranda are given in full.

6. Liddell Hart, *op. cit.*

7. In 1901 General Sigismund von Schlichting, who retired under duress in 1896, published a book called *Moltke's Legacy* in which he objected not only to inflexible operational planning but to inflexible top-command thinking, obviously criticisms directed at Schlieffen. General von der Goltz, one of Germany's best qualified officers, argued vigorously against offensive warfare; General von Bernhardi, a leading military writer, and General von Bülow, whom the younger Moltke replaced as Quartermaster-General of the General Staff in 1904, spoke out in favor of the frontal assault rather than flank envelopment. Ritter, *op. cit.*

8. E. M. Earle, G. A. Craig and F. Gilbert, eds., *Makers of Modern Strategy*, chapter 8: "Moltke and Schlieffen: The Prussian-German School," by Hajo Holborn.

9. General Erich von Ludendorff, *Das Marne-Drama. Der Fall Moltke-Hentsch.*

10. Helmuth von Moltke, *Erinnerungen, Briefe, Dokumenten 1877–1916.*

11. Sewell Tyng, *The Campaign of the Marne 1914.* Written in 1935, this scholarly, detailed and impressively documented work is of value to the professional reader.

12. Ritter, *op. cit.*

13. Ludendorff, *The General Staff and Its Problems.*

14. Ludendorff took command of a brigade in Strasbourg where he planned the *coup de main* against Liége. General Erich von Ludendorff, *My War Memories;* see also John Buchan, *A History of the Great War.*

15. German Army strength increases from 1875 to 1914 are given

in the German General Staff, *Kriegsrüstung und Kriegswirtschaft.*

16. In addition to the trained or ready reserve, the Germans mobilized the *Landwehr* or second line reserve; the *Ersatz*, reserves superfluous to the trained reserve divisions; and the *Landsturm*, youths normally too young for military service and trained and untrained men between thirty-nine and forty-five years. A definitive comparison of total French, German and British forces is given in British Official History (BOH), *France and Belgium, 1914.*

17. The professional reader will find well-illustrated technical studies of German artillery in *Matériels Allemands et Autrichiens.*

18. Models of most of the German and Allied light-infantry weapons and some artillery pieces are on display today in either the Imperial War Museum, London, or La Musée de l'Armée, Paris.

19. Lieutenant General M. von Poseck, *The German Cavalry 1914 in Belgium and France.* General Poseck served as chief of staff, I Cavalry Corps.

20. Marshal of the RAF Sir John Slessor, "Strategy—The German Plan of 1914: In Evolution and Execution" (lecture at the Army Staff College, Camberley, 1933). See also Slessor, *The Great Deterrent.*

21. *Ibid.*

22. The Emperor was actually commander-in-chief, but by tradition the Chief of the Great General Staff took command in the field and issued orders in the Emperor's name. He was supposed to keep the Emperor fully informed and to secure "his decision before taking

important steps." General Erich von Falkenhayn, *General Headquarters, 1914-1916, and its Critical Decisions.*

## CHAPTER 3

1. Bismarck did not want Lorraine but gave in to the elder Moltke who demanded the fortress of Metz for border defense.

2. A complete record of pre-war plans including the full text of Plan XVII is given in the French Official History (FOH), *Les Armées Françaises dans la Grande Guerre,* Vol. I of Tome I; a briefer account is in *The Memoirs of Marshal Joffre.*

3. Earle, Craig and Gilbert, *op. cit.,* chapter 9: "Du Picq and Foch: The French School," by Stefan T. Possony and Etienne Mantoux; an excellent study of Clausewitz' and other influences on Foch is given in B. H. Liddell Hart, *Foch The Man of Orleans;* see also J. F. C. Fuller, *The Decisive Battles of the Western World.*

4. Joffre, *op. cit.*

5. A Catholic, Foch suffered from André's purge. His career was at a perigee in 1906 when Millet, who had taught him at the Ecole de Militaire, intervened on his behalf first with Picquart, Minister of War, then with Clemenceau who eventually appointed him Commandant of the College. Liddell Hart, *Foch.*

6. Introduced in 1898, the French 75-mm. gun created a revolution in artillery. Utilizing a glycerine-filled, very secret cylinder to take the shock of recoil heretofore absorbed by the axletree, the new gun did not have to be reset after each firing. This along with a new mechanized fuse-setter enabled a trained team to fire an unheard-of 25 rounds per minute. F. E. Whitton, *The Marne Campaign.*

7. Joffre, *op. cit.*

8. Moltke made the decision in 1910. Ludendorff, *My War Memories.*

9. Cyril Falls, *The Great War.*

10. Liddell Hart, *A History of the World War 1914-1918.*

11. B. H. Liddell Hart, *Reputations.*

12. The old chief of staff, General Dubail, retained the right to consult the Minister of War directly on certain matters, nor did the new arrangement bring the directors of various arms and services under Joffre's control.

13. Joffre, *op. cit.*

14. Lieutenant Colonel C. à Court Repington, *The First World War 1914-1918.*

15. Originally called a striking force, the name was changed at Repington's suggestion to avoid alarming English radicals.

16. General Huguet, *Britain and the War.*

17. Joffre, *op. cit.*

18. *Ibid.*

19. *Ibid.*

20. FOH, *op. cit.*

21. Unlike the Germans the British units carried no reserve machine guns. Brigadier General Sir James E. Edmonds, *A Short History of World War I.*

22. See note 6 above.

23. General Sir Hubert Gough, *The Fifth Army.*

24. Brigadier E. L. Spears, *Liaison, 1914.* Lieutenant Spears served as BEF liaison officer to the French Fifth Army; his factual yet very witty and brisk writing should delight any reader.

25. Lieutenant General M. B. Burrows, private letter to the author. General Burrows accompanied the BEF to France as the most junior subaltern in the 5th Dragoon Guards, 1st Cavalry Brigade.
26. Maurice Barrès, *The Faith of France.*
27. Philip Guedalla, *Wellington.*

CHAPTER 4

1. Belgian General Staff, *Military Operations of Belgium in Defense of the Country and To Uphold Her Neutrality;* German General Staff, *Lüttich-Namur.*
2. Ludendorff, *My War Memories.*
3. Tyng, *op. cit.*
4. Emil Ludwig, *Kaiser Wilhelm II.*
5. German Official Naval History.
6. Spears, *op. cit.*
7. Joffre, *op. cit.*
8. *Ibid.*
9. A complete record of GQG and army operational and administrative documents is furnished in FOH, annex volumes to Tome 1, vols. 1-3.
10. *Journal of the Royal United Service Institution,* Feb-Nov. 1940: "Alsace-Lorraine in 1914: A Study in Indecision and General Staff Work," by Brigadier General Sir J. E. Edmonds; see also Gerald Campbell, *Verdun to the Vosges.*
11. German Official History, *Der Weltkrieg 1914 bis 1918* (hereafter cited as GOH); Edmonds, op. cit., proves in this well-documented series that German indecision and doubt were not confined to OHL.

12. Field Marshal Lord Ypres French, *1914.*
13. Major General Sir C. E. Callwell, *Field Marshal Sir Henry Wilson—His Life and Diaries;* among the many accounts of these dramatic and sometimes pathetically amusing meetings are Sir George Arthur, *Life of Lord Kitchener;* Philip Magnus, *Kitchener—Portrait of an Imperialist;* W. S. Churchill, *The World Crisis;* Reginald Viscount Esher, *The Tragedy of Lord Kitchener;* Duff Cooper, *Haig.* .
14. Cooper, *op. cit.*
15. Kitchener's complete Letter of Instructions is given in BOH.
16. A good account of the crisis that resulted when the Government attempted to use the army to force the Home Rule Bill in Ulster is given in Callwell, *op. cit.*
17. French, *op. cit.*
18. Cooper, *op. cit.*
19. French, *op. cit.;* Huguet, *op. cit.*
20. Huguet, *op. cit.;* Spears, *op. cit.*
21. *Ibid.*
22. French, *op. cit.*
23. GOH, *op cit.*
24. Belgian General Staff, *op. cit.*
25. GOH, *op. cit.*
26. Generaloberst Alexander von Kluck, *The March on Paris and the Battle of the Marne 1914;* General H. von Kuhl, *Der Marnefeldzug, 1914.*

CHAPTER 5

1. Campbell, *op. cit.*
2. Tyng, *op. cit.*
3. This garrison of two infantry battalions and a battery and half of light guns under Colonel Darché

held out until August 26. Buchan, *op. cit.*

4. Crown Prince Wilhelm, *Meine Erinnerungen aus Deutschlands Heldenkampf.*

5. Tyng, *op. cit.*

6. Colonel A. Grasset, *Neufchâteau.*

7. *Army Quarterly*, April–July 1934: "Foch's Pivot at the Battle of the Marne 1914. The Operations of the Moroccan Division."

8. Joffre, *op. cit.*

9. Tyng, *op. cit.*

10. Spears, *op. cit.*

11. *Ibid.;* Whitton, *The Marne Campaign.*

12. Tyng, *op. cit.*

13. Spears, *op. cit.*

14. Sir John had asked for Herbert Plumer and was annoyed when Kitchener sent out Smith-Dorrien, a veteran infantry officer who had held general officer rank for over half his commissioned service

15. French, *op. cit.*

16. German General Staff, *Die Schlacht bei Mons.*

17. Walter Bloem, *The Advance from Mons 1914.*

18. BOH, *op. cit.;* Spears, *op. cit.*

19. BOH, *op. cit.*

CHAPTER 6

1. Gough, *op. cit.;* Whitton, *The Marne Campaign;* Churchill, *op. cit.*

2. 1041 killed, 2674 wounded, 1058 missing. FOH, *op. cit.*

3. Messimy's attitude is illuminated in a note to Joffre apropos of the Lorraine defeat: "My dear General and Friend: The day before yesterday, a success; yesterday, a repulse. That is war. I have complete faith in the victory of tomorrow. But whatever happens be sure of my unalterable friendship." Joffre, *op. cit.*

4. Joffre had transferred the XVIII Corps to the Fifth Army, the IX Corps to the Fourth Army; one division of the latter and two reservist divisions were now defending.

5. Liddell Hart, *Reputations.*

6. Joffre, *op. cit.*

7. *Ibid.*

8. Spears, *op. cit.*

9. Joffre, *op. cit.*

10. *Ibid.*

11. Edmonds, *op. cit.;* Whitton, *The Marne Campaign.*

12. Generalleutnant Tappen, *Bis zur Marne 1914.*

13. Ludendorff was watching the Second Army fighting its way across the Sambre when the order reached him. Ludendorff, *My War Memories.*

14. Brigadier General John Charteris, *At G.H.Q.:* Arthur Machen claims to have started this legend a month after the battle with a story he wrote that was based on an old legend from earlier wars, when the spirits of English bowmen came back to help their countrymen; he called them "The Angels of Mons." Numerous officers and men, however, spoke and wrote home of the vision at the time of the retreat. It is depicted in a picture in the Mons Museum painted by Marcel Gillis, a local artist.

15. General Sir Horace Smith-Dorrien, *Memories of Forty-Eight Years' Service.*

16. Arthur, *op. cit.*

17. Captain Ernest W. Hamilton, *The First Seven Divisions; Army Quarterly*, April–July 1934: "The Other Side of the Hill: The Night

Attack at Landrecies."
18. BOH, *op. cit.*
19. Smith-Dorrien, *op. cit.*
20. Kluck, *op. cit.* Kluck was further thrown off in his advance from Mons by seeing huge piles of British supplies littering the roadsides; rather than jettisoned equipment from a broken army, these were dumped on orders of General Robertson, QMG, the only way he could feed units whose routes were unknown to him. Spears, *op. cit.*
21. *The Memoirs of Field Marshal the Viscount Montgomery.*

CHAPTER 7

1. Spears, *op. cit.*; Huguet, *op. cit.*
2. Joffre, *op. cit.*
3. Huguet, *op. cit.*
4. *Ibid.*; French, *op. cit.*
5. Henry Wilson did not agree. In the dark days of St. Quentin he allegedly told Sir John French, "The Germans are overhasty. They urge the pursuit too fast. The whole thing is overdone. They are bound to make a big mistake. And then your hour will have come." Esher, *op. cit.*
6. Poincaré stated that Joffre threatened to have him court-martialed and shot. See also Joffre, *op. cit.*; *General M. Gamelin, Manoeuvre et Victoire de la Marne.*
7. He directed Foch to bring Weygand, then second in command of the Fifth Hussars, along as chief of staff. Liddell Hart, *Foch.*
8. Kluck, *op. cit.*
9. *Ibid.* Kluck was more than ever convinced of British defeat by quantities of personal gear found strewn along the roads south of Le Cateau; here again he

erred—on August 28 French ordered the wagons of the II Corps emptied so officers and men could ride; Smith-Dorrien furiously canceled the order but not until the Fourth Division had abandoned most of its kits. Smith-Dorrien, *op. cit.*
10. Kluck, *op. cit.*
11. Field Marshal von Bülow, *Mein Bericht zur Marneschlacht.*
12. Cooper, *op. cit.*; Cameron, *op. cit.*
13. Joachim von Delbrück, *Der Deutsche Krieg in Feldpostbriefen.*
14. Tyng, *op. cit.*, gives an excellent and detailed account of this battle; see also Spears, *op. cit.*; General G. Rouquerol, *La Bataille de Guise*; John Terraine, *Mons.*
15. Callwell, *op. cit.*; Huguet, *op. cit.*; Joffre, *op. cit.* The order was delayed by an administrative error until the next morning, thereby adding to Lanrezac's fury.
16. Arthur, *op. cit.*; see also G. P. Gooch, and H. J. Temperley, eds., *British Documents on the Origin of the War 1894-1914*; Lord Hankey, *The Supreme Command 1914-1918*; Esher, *op. cit.*
17. Arthur, *op. cit.*
18. *Ibid.*
19. *Ibid.*
20. Alan Moorehead, *The White Nile.*
21. Churchill, *op. cit.*
22. Arthur, *op. cit.*
23. Kluck, *op. cit.*

CHAPTER 8

1. This threat stopped the transfer of the XVIII Corps to Paris; instead, Joffre ordered Sarrail to send the IV Corps.
2. FOH, *op. cit.*; the order is translated in full in Tyng, *op. cit.*

3. Joffre, *op. cit.*
4. BOH, *op. cit.*; Huguet, *op. cit.*;
*Journal of the Royal United Service
Institution*, Feb.–Nov. 1919: "The
Fight at Néry," by Major A. F.
Becke.
5. Joffre, *op. cit.*
6. Callwell, *op. cit.*
7. FOH, *op. cit.*
8. Joffre, *op. cit.*; Gamelin, *op. cit.*
9. Wilson wrote in his diary,
"When I got back here [GHQ] I
found that Sir John already had
ordered a retirement, having this
morning specifically stated to the
Governor of Paris that he would
remain on the Marne unless turned
out, and also that he would co-
operate with the Fifth or Sixth
Armies, or both. It is simply heart-
breaking." Callwell, *op. cit.*
10. French, *op. cit.*; Callwell, *op.
cit.*; Gamelin, *op. cit.*
11. FOH, *op. cit.*
12. Kluck, *op. cit.*
13. Buchan, *op. cit.*
14. GOH, *op. cit.*
15. *Ibid.*
16. Kuhl, *op. cit.*
17. Tyng, *op. cit.*; Hauptmann
A. Wirth, *Von der Saale zur Aisne;*
GOH, *op. cit.*
18. *Army Quarterly*, Oct. 1920–
Jan. 1921: "The Scapegoat of the
Battle of the Marne," by Brigadier
General J. E. Edmonds; see also
Kuhl, *op. cit.*

CHAPTER 9

1. Bloem, *op. cit.*
2. Spears, *op. cit.*
3. Esher, *op. cit.*
4. GOH, *op. cit.*
5. Pétain was promoted for an
excellent job at St. Quentin. Somewhere between St. Quentin and the
Marne he stopped in a village

where an elderly spinster found
some insignia on a tunic of a dead
relative and sewed them on his
tunic. Philip Guedalla, *The Two
Marshals;* G. Bolton, *Pétain.*
6. U. S. National Archives,
Records of the War Department
General Staff: "Report Number
32: Progress of the War," by
Major Spencer Cosby.
7. FOH, *op. cit.*
8. GOH, *op. cit.*
9. *Blackwood's Magazine*, Feb.
1915: "Diary of a Subaltern."
10. BOH, *op. cit.*
11. General Pierre Héring, *La
Vie Exemplaire de Philippe Pétain;*
Liddell Hart, *Reputations.*
12. FOH, *op. cit.*
13. FOH, *op. cit.*; Colonel A.
Grasset, *La Bataille des Deux
Morins;* Tyng, *op. cit.*
14. FOH, *op. cit.*; GOH, *op. cit.*;
Generaloberst Freiherr von Hausen, *Erinnerungen an der Marne;*
Generalmajor Artur Baumgarten-
Crusius, *Die Marneschlacht 1914.*
15. This order was signed by
General Tulff von Tscheppe, commanding the VIII Corps. Whitton,
*The Marne Campaign.*
16. Delbrück, *op. cit.*
17. GOH, *op. cit.*; BOH, *op. cit.*
18. General von Einem, *Erinnerungen eines Soldaten 1853-1933.*

CHAPTER 10

1. GOH, *op. cit.*
2. FOH, *op. cit.*; Tyng, *op. cit.*
3. José Roussel-Lépine, *Les
Champs de l'Ourcq.*
4. Christian Mallet, *Impressions
and Experiences of a French
Trooper, 1914-15.*
5. Not only the French government but nearly 100,000 citizens
evacuated Paris. Of the diplomatic

corps only the staffs of the Spanish and American Embassies remained. U. S. National Archives, Records of the War Department General Staff: Cosby, *op. cit.*
  6. Commandant Henri Carré, *La Véritable Histoire des Taxis de la Marne.*
  7. Charteris, *op. cit.*
  8. Frederic Coleman, *From Mons to Ypres with General French.*
  9. FOH, *op. cit.;* Tyng, *op. cit.;* Charles Le Goffic, *General Foch at the Marne.*
  10. U. S. National Archives, Records of the War Department General Staff: Cosby, *op. cit.*
  11. Barrès, *op. cit.*
  12. GOH, *op. cit.*
  13. Count Alfred von Schlieffen, *Cannae* (Holborn's translation).
  14. Liddell Hart, *Reputations.*
  15. Moltke, *op. cit.*
  16. U. S. National Archives, Records of the War Department General Staff: "Report Number 33: Visit to the Battlefields," by Major Spencer Cosby.
  17. FOH, *op. cit.*
  18. Joffre, *op. cit.*

CHAPTER I I

  1. GOH, *op. cit.*
  2. *Ibid.*
  3. *Army Quarterly,* Oct. 1933–Jan. 1934: Edmonds, *op cit.;* Ludendorff, *Das Marne-Drama. Der Fall Moltke–Hentsch;* GOH, *op. cit.;* Tyng, *op. cit.*
  4. Mallet, *op. cit.;* see also FOH, *op. cit.;* Kluck, *op. cit.*
  5. Coleman, *op. cit.*
  6. FOH, *op. cit.;* Oberstleutnant Eugen Bircher, *Die Krisis in der Marneschlacht.*
  7. Delbrück, *op. cit.*
  8. FOH, *op. cit.*

  9. Kluck, *op. cit.*
  10. BOH, *op. cit.*
  11. Earle, Craig, Gilbert: Possony and Mantoux, *op. cit.*
  12. Tyng, *op. cit.*
  13. Grasset, *op. cit.;* FOH, *op. cit.*
  14. Joffre, *op. cit.*

CHAPTER I 2

  1. *Army Quarterly:* Edmonds, *op. cit.;* Ludendorff, *Das Marne-Drama;* GOH, *op. cit.;* Tyng, *op. cit.*
  2. Bloem, *op. cit.*
  3. *Ibid.*
  4. *Army Quarterly,* April-July, 1934, *op. cit.*
  5. Buchan, *op. cit.*
  6. Bülow, *op. cit.*
  7. GOH, *op. cit.*
  8 Kluck, *op. cit.*
  9. The château was rebuilt but its shell-marked walls still stand. An enormous war memorial, a sort of abstract phoenix, stands where the French battalion assembled for the first assault.
  10. GOH, *op. cit.*
  11. *Ibid.*
  12. Barrès, *op. cit.*
  13. *Journal of the Royal United Service Institution,* Feb.–Nov. 1934: "Air Reconnaissance in Open Warfare," by Wing Commander (now Marshal of the RAF Sir) John Slessor.
  14. Grasset, *op. cit.;* FOH, *op. cit.;* Tyng, *op. cit.*
  15. Joffre, *op. cit.*
  16. Moltke, *op. cit.*

CHAPTER I 3

  1. GOH, *op. cit.*
  2. *Ibid.*
  3. FOH, *op. cit.*

4. *Ibid.*
5. BOH, *op. cit.*
6. Joffre, *op. cit.*
7. They escaped with 506,000 francs, all the Mayor could scrape up. U. S. National Archives, Records of the War Department General Staff: "Report Number 36: Visit to the Battlefield," by Major Spencer Cosby.
8. *Ibid.*
9. FOH, *op. cit.*

CHAPTER 14

1. FOH, *op. cit.*
2. BOH, *op. cit.*
3. U. S. National Archives, Records of the War Department General Staff: "Report Number 45: Battle of the Marne," by Major Spencer Cosby.
4. Thus excluding three infantry corps, a reserve division and the *Ersatz* divisions which were not Bavarian. *Journal of the Royal United Service Institution*, Feb.–Nov. 1940: Edmonds, *op. cit.*
5. Falkenhayn, *op. cit.*
6. The phrase seems to have evolved because Germany trumpeted to the world her continued possession of French territory while she was conducting a "strategic adjustment"; simultaneously, and to Joffre's understandable

disgust, the French government played down the victory in order to prevent false optimism and "save the nerves of the country."
7. *Army Quarterly*, April 1958: "Hitler and Dunkirk," by Captain Robert B. Asprey.
8. Colonel A. M. Henniker, *Transportation on the Western Front 1914–1918.*
9. Poseck, *op. cit.*
10. Henniker, *op. cit.*
11. Kluck, *op. cit.*
12. Henniker, *op. cit.*
13. *Ibid.*
14. *Ibid.*
15. Joffre, *op. cit.*
16. Kluck, *op. cit.*
17. *Ibid.*
18. *Ibid.*
19. Bloem, *op. cit.*
20. *Ibid.*
21. Liddell Hart, *A History of the World War.*
22. Ludwig Reiners, *The Lamps Went Out in Europe.*
23. Ludendorff, *Das Marne-Drama. Der Fall Moltke-Hentsch.*

CHAPTER 15

1. Arthur, *op. cit.*
2. FOH, *op. cit.;* Huguet, *op. cit.*
3. Joffre, *op. cit.*
4. Tyng, *op. cit.*

# BIBLIOGRAPHY
## & INDEX

# BIBLIOGRAPHY

Arminius, *pseud.*, *From Sarajevo to the Rhine* (London, Hutchinson, 1933).

Arthur, Sir George, *Life of Lord Kitchener* (London, Macmillan, 1920). Vol. III of 3 vols.

*Army Quarterly* (London):

Oct. 1920–Jan. 1921: "The Scapegoat of the Battle of the Marne, 1914. Lieutenant Colonel Hentsch and the Order for the German Retreat," by Brigadier General J. E. Edmonds.

Apr.–July 1934: "Foch's Pivot at the Battle of the Marne 1914. The Operations of the Moroccan Division"; "Battle of the Marne 1914: The Night Attack at Landrecies, 25th August."

Oct. 1933–Jan. 1934: "The French Official Account of the Marne 1914—Franchet d'Esperey's Army."

April 1958: "Hitler and Dunkirk," by Captain Robert B. Asprey.

Asprey, Robert B., *The Panther's Feast* (New York, Putnam, 1959).

Asquith, H. H., *The Genesis of the War* (London, Cassell, 1923).

Barrès, Maurice, *The Faith of France* (New York, Houghton Mifflin, 1918).

Bartz, Karl, *Die Deutschen von Paris* (Berlin, Bischoff, 1934).

Baumgarten-Crusius, Generalmajor Artur, *Die Marneschlacht 1914* (Leipzig, Lippold, 1919).

——, *Deutsche Heerführung im Marnefeldzug, 1914* (Berlin, Scherl, 1921).

Bavarian General Staff, *Die Schlacht in Lothringen* (Munich, Schick, 1929).

Belgian General Staff, *Military Operations of Belgium in Defense of the Country and To Uphold Her Neutrality* (London, Collingridge).

Berger-Levrault, eds., *Matériels Allemands et Autrichiens—A Grande Puissance* (Paris, Berger-Levrault, 1921).

Bircher, Oberstleutnant Eugen, *Die Krisis in der Marneschlacht* (Bern, Bircher, 1927).

Bloem, Walter, *The Advance from Mons 1914* (London, Peter Davies, 1923).

Bolton, J. G. R., *Pétain* (London, Allen and Unwin, 1957).

Bouman, P. J., *Revolution of the Lonely* (New York, McGraw-Hill, 1954).

Buchan, John, *A History of the Great War* (London, Thos. Nelson, 1921). Vol. I of 4 vols.

Bülow, Field Marshal von, *Mein Bericht zur Marneschlacht* (Berlin, Scherl, 1919).

Callwell, Major General Sir C. E., *Field Marshal Sir Henry Wilson—His Life and Diaries* (London, Cassell, 1927). Vol. I of 2 vols.

Cameron, James, *1914* (London, Cassell, 1959).

Campbell, Gerald, *Verdun to the Vosges* (London, Arnold, 1916).

Carré, Commandant Henri, *La Véritable Histoire des Taxis de la Marne* (Paris, Libraire Chapelot, 1921).

Charteris, Brigadier General John, *At G.H.Q.* (London, Cassell, 1931).

Churchill, W. S., *The World Crisis 1911–1918* (London, Butterworth, 1923).

——, *Great Contemporaries* (London, Butterworth, 1937).

Coblentz, Paul, *The Silence of Sarrail* (London, Hutchinson, 1930).

Cochenhausen, General von, *Von Scharnhorst zu Schlieffen* (Berlin, Mittler, 1933).

Coleman, Frederic, *From Mons to Ypres with General French* (New York, Dodd, Mead, 1916).

Cooper, Duff, *Haig* (London, Faber and Faber, 1935). Vol. I of 2 vols.

Corbett-Smith, A., *The Marne—and After* (London, Cassell, 1917).

Cosby, Major Spencer, *see* U.S. National Archives.

Delbrück, Joachim von, *Der Deutsche Krieg in Feldpostbriefen* (Munich, Georg Müller, 1915–17).

Earle, E. M., Craig, G. A., Gilbert, F., eds., *Makers of Modern Strategy* (Princeton, N.J., Princeton University Press, 1943).

Edmonds, Brigadier General Sir James E., *Military Operations: France and Belgium, 1914* (British Official History) (London, Macmillan, 1933).

——, *A Short History of World War I* (London, Oxford University Press, 1951).

Einem, General von, *Erinnerungen eines Soldaten 1855–1933* (Leipzig, Köhler, 1933).

Esher, Reginald Viscount, *The Tragedy of Lord Kitchener* (London, John Murray, 1921).

Eyck, Erich, *Bismarck and the German Empire* (London, Allen and Unwin, 1950).

Falkenhayn, General Erich von, *General Headquarters, 1914–1916, and its Critical Decisions* (London, Hutchinson, 1919).

Falls, Cyril, *The Great War* (New York, Putnam, 1959).

French, Field Marshal Lord Ypres, *1914* (London, Constable, 1919).

French General Staff, *Les Armées Françaises dans la Grande Guerre* (Paris, Imprimerie Nationale, 1922–1934). Tome I: 3 vols. and annex vols.

Foch, Marshal Ferdinand, *Mémoires* (Paris, Plon, 1931).

Fuller, Major General J. F. C., *The Decisive Battles of the Western World* (London, Eyre and Spottiswoode, 1956). Vol. III of 3 vols.

Galliéni, Marshal Joseph Simon, *Mémoires* (Paris, Payot, 1920).

Gamelin, General M., *Manoeuvre et Victoire de la Marne* (Paris, Bern and Grasset, 1954).

German General Staff, *Lüttich–Namur* (Oldenburg, Stalling, 1918).

——, *Die Schlacht bei Mons* (Oldenburg, Stalling, 1918).

——, *Der Weltkrieg 1914 bis 1918. Die Militärischen Operationen zu Lande* (Berlin, Mittler). Vols. I, III, IV, V.

——, *Kriegsrüstung und Kriegswirtschaft* (Berlin, 1930).

Gooch, G. P., Temperley, H. J., eds., *British Documents on the Origins of the War 1894–1914* (London, HMSO, 1926). Vol. XI.

Görlitz, Walter, *The German General Staff* (New York, Praeger, 1959).
Gough, General Sir Hubert, *The Fifth Army* (London, Hodder and Stoughton, 1931).
Grasset, Colonel A., *Neufchâteau* (Paris, Berger-Levrault, 1930).
———, *La Bataille des Deux Morins* (Paris, Payot, 1934).
Grey, Viscount, *Twenty-Five Years* (London, Hodder and Stoughton, 1925). 2 vols.
Guedalla, Philip, *The Two Marshals* (London, Hodder and Stoughton, 1943).
———, *Wellington* (New York, Harper, 1931).
Hamilton, Captain Ernest W., *The First Seven Divisions* (London, Hurst and Blackett, 1916).
Hankey, Lord, *The Supreme Command 1914-1918* (London, Allen and Unwin, 1961). Vol. I of 2 vols.
Hausen, General Freiherr von, *Erinnerungen an den Marnefeldzug 1914* (Berlin, Köhler, 1919).
Henniker, Colonel A. M., *Transportation on the Western Front 1914-1918* (British Official History) (London, HMSO, 1937).
Hérring, General Pierre, *La Vie Exemplaire de Philippe Pétain* (Paris, Editions Paris-Livres, 1956).
Huguet, General, *Britain and the War* (London, Cassell, 1928).
Joffre, The Ex-Crown Prince of Germany, Foch, Ludendorff, *The Two Battles of the Marne* (London, Butterworth, 1927).
Joffre, Marshal, *The Memoirs of Marshal Joffre* (London, Bles, 1932). Vol. I of 2 vols.
*Journal of the Royal United Service Institution* (London):
    Feb.-Nov. 1914: "The Fight at Néry September 1st, 1914," by Major A. F. Becke.
    Nov. 1934: "Air Reconnaissance in Open Warfare," by Wing Commander (now Marshal of the RAF Sir) John Slessor.
    Feb.-Nov. 1940: "Alsace-Lorraine in 1914 (A Study in Indecision and German Staff Work)," by Brigadier General Sir James E. Edmonds.
Kluck, Generaloberst Alexander von, *The March on Paris and the Battle of the Marne, 1914* (London, Edward Arnold, 1923).
Kuhl, General H. von, *Der Deutsche Generalstab*, (Berlin, Mittler, 1920).

———, *Der Marnefeldzug, 1914* (Berlin, Mittler, 1921).

Le Goffic, Charles, *General Foch at the Marne* (London, Dent, 1918).

Liddell Hart, B. H., *Reputations* (London, Murray, 1928).

———, *Foch: The Man of Orleans* (London, Eyre and Spottiswoode, 1931).

———, *A History of the World War 1914-1918* (London, Faber and Faber, 1934).

———, *Strategy, the Indirect Approach* (London, Faber and Faber, 1954).

Ludendorff, General Erich, *My War Memories 1914-1918* (London, Hutchinson, 1919). Vol. I of 2 vols.

———, *The General Staff and Its Problems* (London, Hutchinson, 1920). Vol. I of 2 vols.

———, *Das Marne-Drama. Der Fall Moltke-Hentsch* (Munich, Ludendorff's Verlag, 1934).

Ludwig, Emil, *Kaiser Wilhelm II* (New York, Putnam, 1926).

———, *Bismarck* (London, Allen and Unwin, 1927).

———, *July 1914* (New York, Putnam, 1929).

Lyet, Capitaine P., *Joffre et Galliéni à la Marne* (Paris, Berger-Levrault, 1938).

Machen, Arthur, *The Angels of Mons* (London, Simpkin, 1915).

Magnus, Philip, *Kitchener—Portrait of an Imperialist* (London, John Murray, 1958).

Mallet, Christian, *Impressions and Experiences of a French Trooper, 1914-1915* (London, Constable, 1916).

Moltke, Helmut von, *Erinnerungen, Briefe, Dokumente 1877-1916* (Stuttgart, Der Kommende Tag, 1922).

Montgomery, Field Marshal the Viscount, *The Memoirs of Field Marshal the Viscount Montgomery* (London, Collins, 1958).

Moorehead, Alan, *The White Nile* (London, Hamish Hamilton, 1960).

*National Review* (London):
　　Oct. 1920: "The Crisis of the Marne 1914," by D. Forester and E. W. Shepherd.

Perris, G. H., *The Battle of the Marne* (London, Hodder and Stoughton, 1920).

Poseck, Lieutenant General M. von, *The German Cavalry 1914 in Belgium and France* (Berlin, Mittler, 1923).

Reiners, Ludwig, *The Lamps Went Out in Europe* (New York: Pantheon, 1955).

Repington, Lieutenant Colonel C. à Court, *The First World War 1914–1918* (London, Constable, 1920). Vol. I of 2 vols.

Ritter, Gerhard, *The Schlieffen Plan* (New York, Praeger, 1958).

Robertson, Field Marshal Sir William, *From Private to Field Marshal* (London, Constable, 1921).

Roussel-Lépine, José, *Les Champs de l'Ourcq* (Paris, Plon, 1919).

Rupprecht, Crown Prince, *Mein Kriegstagebuch* (Munich, Deutscher National Verlag, 1928).

Schlieffen, Count Alfred von, *Cannae* (Berlin, 1925).

Slessor, Marshal of the RAF Sir John, *The Great Deterrent* (London, Cassell, 1957).

Smith-Dorrien, General Sir Horace, *Memories of Forty-Eight Years Service* (London, John Murray, 1925).

Spears, E. L., *Liaison, 1914* (London: Heinemann, 1930).

Stein, General von, *A War Minister and His Work* (London, Sheffington).

Tappen, Generalleutnant, *Bis zur Marne 1914* (Berlin, Oldenburg, 1920).

Terrain, John, *Mons* (New York, Macmillan, 1960).

Tyng, Sewell, *The Campaign of the Marne 1914* (New York, Longmans, Green, 1935).

U.S. National Archives, Records of the War Department of the General Staff: Records WCD 8690: 32-33, 36, 41, 46, 48-49, 72, 91-92, 94, by Major Spencer Cosby, USA.

Whitton, Lieutenant Colonel F. E., *The Marne Campaign* (London, Constable, 1917).

———, *Moltke* (London, Constable, 1921).

Wilhelm, Crown Prince, *Der Marne-Feldzug 1914* (Berlin, Dob, 1926).

Wirth, Hauptmann A., *Von der Saale zur Aisne* (Leipzig, Hesse and Becker, 1920).

# INDEX